Buying Time
a play in two acts
by

Michael Weller

SAMUEL FRENCH, INC.

Also by Michael Weller

ABROAD

AT HOME

THE BALLAD OF SOAPY SMITH

FISHING

GHOST ON FIRE

LAKE NO BOTTOM

LOOSE ENDS

MOONCHILDREN

NOW THERE'S JUST THE THREE OF US

SPLIT

SPOILS OF WAR

****

Maxim Gorkey's
BARBARIANS

translated by
Michael Weller

Buying Time by *Michael Weller*

*opened November 1, 2000 at the Hypothetical Theatre
(Artistic Director Amy Feinberg)
in the 14th Street Y Theatre of The Educational Alliance,
344 East 14th Street, New York City.*

*It was extended in a commercial production
in the same space a month later by
producers Jerry Lasky, Jerry Rosengarten and Susann Brinkley
with some new cast members (indicated in brackets).*

Cast

Carter VanZant	Mark Dold (Nathan M. White)
Lane Scotto/Waiter	David Ari
Hal Gold	Jeff Kronson
Margot Buonovecchio	Jennifer Trimble
Pete Water	Patrick Boll
Bennett Traube	Lee Sellers
Del Gregorian	Tibor Feldman
Max Lasker/Laird Sutter	Chuck Montgomery
Abe Einhorn	Evan Thompson (Gene Terruso)
Jobeth Traube	Monique Fowler (Dierdre O'Connell & Catherine Dowling)
Christine Martel	Jennifer Gibbs
Carlos	Antonio del Rosario
Becky Sutter	Irene McDonnell
Troy Sutter	Andy Powers
Voice Over	Catherine Dowling
Director	Amy Feinberg
Set Design	Mark Symczak
Costume Design	T. Michael Hall
Sound Design	Tim Cramer
Lighting Design	Jeff Croiter
Technical Direction	Bill Mitchell
Production Stage Manager	Nicole Mole
Assistant Stage Manager	Margaret A. Flanagan
Lighting Associate	Kevin J. Hardy

Setting: Mesa, Arizona

Time: The Mid 1990s

Buying Time

a play in two acts
by

Michael Weller

SAMUEL FRENCH, INC.

45 West 25th Street   7623 Sunset Boulevard
NEW YORK 10010   HOLLYWOOD 90046
LONDON   *TORONTO*

Copyright © 2002 by Michael Weller

ALL RIGHTS RESERVED

CAUTION: Professionals and amateurs are hereby warned that BUYING TIME is subject to a royalty. It is fully protected under the copyright laws of the United States of America, the British Commonwealth, including Canada, and all other countries of the Copyright Union. All rights, including professional, amateur, motion pictures, recitation, lecturing, public reading, radio broadcasting, television, and the rights of translation into foreign languages are strictly reserved. In its present form the play is dedicated to the reading public only.

The amateur live stage performance rights to BUYING TIME are controlled exclusively by Samuel French, Inc. and royalty arrangements and licenses must be secured well in advance of presentation. PLEASE NOTE that amateur royalty fees are set upon application in accordance with your producing circumstances. When applying for a royalty quotation and license please give us the number of performances intended, dates of production, your seating capacity and admission fee. Royalties are payable one week before the opening performance of the play to Samuel French, Inc., at 45 West 25th Street, New York, NY 10010; or at 7623 Sunset Blvd., Hollywood, CA 90046, or to Samuel French (Canada), Ltd., 100 Lombard Street, Lower Level, Toronto, Ontario, Canada M5C 1M3.

Royalty of the required amount must be paid whether the play is presented for charity or gain and whether or not admission is charged.

Stock royalty quoted on application to Samuel French, Inc.

For all other rights than those stipulated above, apply to Joyce Ketay Agency, 1501 Broadway, New York, NY 10036.

Particular emphasis is laid on the question of amateur or professional readings, permission and terms for which must be secured in writing from Samuel French, Inc.

Copying from this book in whole or in part is strictly forbidden by law, and the right of performance is not transferable.

Whenever the play is produced the following notice must appear on all programs, printing and advertising for the play: "Produced by special arrangement with Samuel French, Inc."

Due authorship credit must be given on all programs, printing and advertising for the play.

ISBN 0 573 62817 3   Printed in U.S.A.   #4233

No one shall commit or authorize any act or omission by which the copyright of, or the right to copyright, this play may be impaired.

No one shall make any changes in this play for the purpose of production.

Publication of this play does not imply availability for performance. Both amateurs and professionals considering a production are *strongly* advised in their own interests to apply to Samuel French, Inc., for written permission before starting rehearsals, advertising, or booking a theatre.

No part of this book may be reproduced, stored in a retrieval system, or transmitted in any form, by any means, now known or yet to be invented, including mechanical, electronic, photocopying, recording, videotaping, or otherwise, without the prior written permission of the publisher.

IMPORTANT BILLING AND CREDIT REQUIREMENTS

All producers of BUYING TME *must* give credit to the Author of the Play in all programs distributed in connection with performances of the Play and in all instances in which the title of the Play appears for purposes of advertising, publicizing or otherwise exploiting the Play and/or a production. The name of the Author *must* also appear on a separate line, on which no other name appears, immediately following the title, and *must* appear in size of type not less than fifty percent the size of the title type. Additionally, credit must be given to the original producer of the Play in a conspicuous place in all programs distributed in connection with performances of the Play.

Billing *must* be substantially as follows:

(NAME OF PRODUCER)
presents

BUYING TIME

by

Michael Weller

Produced in New York by the
Hypothetical Theatre Company, Inc.

Seattle Repertory Theatre
Daniel Sullivan, Artistic Director

BUYING TIME
A WORLD PREMIERE BY MICHAEL WELLER
Opening date: January 27, 1996

Director	Robert Egan
Scenic Designer	David Jenkins
Costume Designer	Rose Pederson
Light Designer	Rick Paulsen
Composer/Sound Designer	David Pascal

Cast (in alphabetical order)

Troy Sutter/Wythe	Andrew Boyer
Christine Martel	Kristin Flanders
Jobeth Traube	Katie Forgette
Bennett Traube	Mark Harelik
Lane Scotto/Waiter	Peter Lohnes
Abe Einhorn	William Biff McGuire
Max Lasker/Laird Sutter	Stephen Markle
Margot Buonovecchio	Marianne Owen
Del Gregorian	John Procaccino
Hal Gold	Rick Tutor
Becky Sutter/Rita	Lauren Tewes
Carter VanZant	Christopher Evan Welch
Peter Water	R. Hamilton Wright

Stage Manager	Stephanie Hagerty
Assistant Stage Manager	Jennifer Kimball
Stage Management Intern	Cindy Kocher
Directing Intern	Josefin O'Brien
Assistant Lighting Designers	Jay Strevey
	Claudia Gallagher
Assistant to the Playwright	Hunt Holman
Flight Consultant	Geoffrey Alm

ACT I

Scene 1 / Hotel Room — Downtown Mesa

(On a bed pulled to center-room CARTER VanZANT and LANE SCOTTO, both in their late 20s, stand chug-a-lugging quart bottles of beer while two lawyers in their mid-40s, HAL GOLD and MARGOT BUONAVECCHIO, cheer them on.
(PETE WATER [40s], his back to us, splits his attention between the drinking contest and a TV, which he watches with the volume on very low.
CARTER, done, brandishes his bottle overhead.)

CARTER. *(with a southern lilt)* The winnah, VanZant!
LANE. *(lowering his unfinished bottle)* I appeal this result —
MARGOT. *(playing judge)* On what grounds...?
CARTER. — bullshit, Scotto! —
LANE. — VanZant's drinking candy ass Lite beer whereas mine, check it out, is a manly high testosterone lager —
CARTER. Your honor, he just proved my point; litigators make piss poor losers!
OTHERS. *(ad lib, except for PETE)* Look out, VanZant! Take it back! You're outnumbered! You're drinking our booze — !
CARTER. You courtroom cowboys may be the big swinging dicks in this firm but when push comes to shove you're all bunch of closet weenies who can't drink fight or make love in the afternoon.
LANE. — And *I* say "Lite" beer is the perfect symbol of all you get-a-life smurfs in the Corporate section —

(PETE and HAL start razzing LANE until —)

MARGOT. — Girls, girls, let's not quarrel among fiends.

(The outburst is interrupted by the arrival of DEL GREGORIAN,

Managing Partner of D&R, a florid, round-faced man with high blood pressure.)

DEL. *(over everyone)* What the hell's going on in here, I heard you all the way down at the elevators!

(BENNETT hurries in; energetic, restless movements.)

BEN. *(loud)* Guys, guys, time to focus, we have to plan strategy for the press. *(to PETE)* We on yet?
PETE. Still the game, Astros up two. *(HAL starts chanting "Bennett-Bennett-Bennett Traube, Bennett-Bennett-Bennett Traube." The chant is taken up by ALL until BENNETT holds up his hands.)* Alright, guys, quiet down. They're waiting for us down there. The ballroom's a media circus, I saw network guys —
DEL. *(to CARTER)* VanZant, watch the hall, tell us when Max is coming.

(VanZANT obeys as BENNETT addresses the room.)

BEN. This victory can work for us big time, I'm talking major exposure, national coverage, and best of all —
HAL. Free!
BEN. Right! So when we work the ballroom, here's the company spin: A) We at Donne & Russo deeply regret any personal pain to the Governor's family and friends as a result of his forced resignation, but, B) Our law firm is proud that we upheld the state constitution over electoral tampering and —
DEL. The system works, *that*'s what we sell; no one is above the law!
HAL. Not even lawyers?!

(Appreciative laughter.)

BEN. We won't go *that* far.
DEL. The Governor's out of office, but he still has friends in high places, some of 'em valued clients of ours, so —

PETE. — "Proud but humble"; we got the picture, Del.
CARTER. *(at the door)* Here comes Max.
BEN. Lights out!

(Lights out, then the TV. Darkness. A pause. From outside the door a booming voice sings.)

MAX. *(off:)* FOR HE'S A JOLLY GOOD FEL....LOW — *(The door bursts open silhouetting MAX.)* WHICH NOBODY CAN DENY...! Surprise!

(MAX, wry and gruff, flips on the lights.)

HAL. A true gentleman would pretend not to know we're here.
MAX. A) Who's a gentleman and B) what are we drinking?
BEN. *(from the bed)* Max, kindly step up here a moment.
MAX. *(siren)* Nee-ner-nee-ner, Bullshit Alert; everyone duck!
BEN. *(riffing on an orotund toastmaster)* Ladies & Gentlemen, we all know Max Lasker as a great lawyer, architect of today's historic victory, and withall a man of many parts; four star chili chef, amateur astronomer, practical joker — qualities another law firm might deem exceptional, but we at Donne & Russo we take for granted in even the lowliest summer associate — *(Cheers, ad libs, high spirits.)* — What has never been told is how Max, like so many of us at D&R, did not set out to practice law in Mesa, but heading west one day for where was it — San Francisco?

OTHERS. Boooo!

BEN. ... he stopped overnight in this New Jerusalem of the west, and it was love at first sight; the clean air, the friendly pace —

CARTER. The dust —

HAL. The heat —

PETE. Coyotes eating your house pets —

BEN. He's seen this once sleepy cow town grow to a thriving metropolis of one million people; and a firm of fifteen partners become *eighty-seven. (Raucous ad libs, HAL hums a "March of Time" theme.)* But — Quiet! — in these 20 years of dizzying growth, has Max remained true to the sacred words of our clan god Eagle-of-Legal when he created First Lawyer from the dung of a mountain goat...? *(All shout objections; retreating:)* It was a *nice* goat. Very clean. Margot! *(MARGOT passes him a small shiny red shopping bag. BENNETT pulls out a tee-shirt.)* We had the holy words inscribed on this tribal vestment: *(BENNETT unfolds a DONNE & RUSSO tee-shirt to show lettered across the front: YENOM EROM.)* "Yenom Erom," which, in the great tradition of legal jargon makes sense only when you read it backwards —

ALL. *(pause, then in unison:)* MORE MONEY! *(ad lib)* Put it on, Max. Speech! We love you, Max.

(BENNETT slips the tee shirt on MAX over his jacket to much cheering.)

MAX. First I'd like to thank our Managing Partner, the indomitable Del Gregorian, for letting us run with this case. *(Cheers. MAX suddenly continues, oddly serious.)* What a night! We nailed a true shitheel, and with nothing to gain beyond upholding the public interest. Good for the soul, a victory like this. Justice; what a concept! Think about it! One place under the sun where the mighty and the humble stand equal. If I had to argue for God's existence I'd say "who else could conceive a creature that invented something as perfect as The Law?" And I'd argue there's a Satan because who else would go and invent lawyers to fuck it all up? *(MAX's mood puzzles everyone.)* Anyway, you're a crack team, D&R's been a great place *(covering:) always* been a great place to do law, and I'm proud as hell of every one of you. Thank you.

(To break the suddenly awkward mood, BENNETT sings "For He's a Jolly Good Fellow." The others join in.)

DEL. Okay, everyone, to the ballroom! And remember with the press —
PETE. Proud but humble!!!
DEL. Hell of a job, guys. You earned this one.
MARGOT. *(tartly, catching his tone)* Thanks, Del!

(The others laugh and carry on as they file out.)

DEL. Don't keep 'em waiting downstairs.

(DEL exits and MAX starts to follow him.)

BEN. Is the tee-shirt a fashion statement?
MAX. *(notes that he's wearing it)* Whoops.

(MAX removes it.)

BEN. *(watching MAX, puzzled)* Kind of a serioso speech, Lasker. Not our typical Merry Max.

MAX. Middle age, what can I tell ya? I had a pony tail when we started here, remember?

(Pause. They smile, then break into whoops.)

BEN. We *did* it, Max, oh man, I've had highs before but — the Governor of the state, for fuck's sake. We did it, we saved the firm!

MAX. We saved *what*?!

BEN. Pro bono. Rule 7.

MAX. Dream on, Mister T.

BEN. Come on, man, the corporate guys were bean-counting our time sheets up the wazoo on this one, if we'd lost against the governor, they'd've been all over us like a bad suit, "You litigators wasted two thousand hours on a political vendetta, that's our Christmas bonus, Rule 7 is killing this firm, blah-blah-blah." Instead; cover story, *American Lawyer*; *Time Magazine* feature, "Donne & Russo, lawyers with a vision ..." Corporate can't bitch at that result.

MAX. Guess who's boycotting the party, Hopalong; half the corporate section.

BEN. *(beat)* Okay, it's not their victory, fuck 'em.

MAX. *(growing anger)* It's the whole firm's victory. We should all be together down there, damn it!

BEN. You're beautiful when you're angry.

MAX. I'm serious, Bennett. Ten years ago they wouldn't have dared pull something like this. Five, even.

BEN. Let 'em boycott, let 'em sulk, let 'em crawl back in a hole and write contracts and badmouth litigators 'til the moon turns blue, as long as they can't get their hands on pro bono. *(a toast)* To our Holy of Holies, Bylaw 7, the public good, *pro bono publicum!*

MAX. *(stops him)* I came to Mesa to get laid, d'I ever tell you? True story, and not a word of this to Maia, cause we were already engaged. I had this job interview in Frisco, and an old girlfriend from law school calls, "Hey, Maxie, drive through Mesa on your way west, and we'll get it on."

BEN. "Get it on!" God, I love Colonial English!

MAX. So we're in bed getting biological, and she starts in about this place where she's a summer associate; D&R, some little weird-ass firm that *pays* you for pro bono work, up to 20 percent of billable hours, and it's in the fuckin' *bylaws*, Rule 7 it's called, and I'm going "this chick is stoned, what's she talking about, legal aid or something" — she's grabbing my hand, putting it places but I'm getting curious about this firm of hers, like "who pays for these free hours?" and she's going "Harder Max, faster," but I'm very interested now, like "How does it work, the rainmakers subsidize the freebies, and they're *okay* with this?" She's making these moany-gurgling noises but now I'm going nuts trying to work it out; I mean, are these guys for-real grown up attorneys, or are we talking Larry-the-Lawyer wannabees who passed their bar exam after five tries? So next morning I swing by the place to check it out, and hallelujah! Everything she said was true. It was legal paradise, man. I applied on the spot.

BEN. Question; Did you satisfy the lady that night?

MAX. Answer; Does the Pope wear condoms?

BEN. Next question. Why this story?

MAX. The new guys, they're different. Social action means nothing to them. *Pro bono's* some historical curiosity, a quaint collectable from the Golden Age of Law. All the youngbloods dream about is a Lamborghini with wraparound stereo, tilt-back seats and a blond shiksa wearing a perfume called "Portfolio."

BEN. That's better. For a minute I thought you'd checked your sense of humor at the door.

MAX. The Governor was our swan song, B-man.

BEN. *(very concerned)* Max, what is *with* you tonight?

MAX. D'you see his face when they read the verdict? He was

smirking. He lost a skirmish, but he knows he'll win the war. We're the dinosaurs. The new guys are fast and glib and fearless, and we're in their way. Just to hold the line against 'em from now on ... I don't have the energy. I'm tired, Bennett. Okay? I want time with Maia and the kids. I want my life back.

BEN. Don't let this be going where I think it is!

MAX. *(beat)* I bought into a one horse operation, Livingston Montana. Wills, land titles, DWI; routine stuff; oil change, spark plugs ...

BEN. But you're the next Managing Partner, it's a given. The firm is *ours* now, we can take it anywhere we want.

MAX. If we'd lost, I'd hang in a while till things calmed down. But this victory buys you time; you want the firm, take it.

BEN. *(beat)* No, man. There's a trust here. Del let us run with this case for one reason only; he knew you'd be Managing Partner after him, and you could keep the corporate section in line. *(then:)* What'll change your mind? A year off with pay? A bigger Christmas bonus? The firm needs you, Max.

MAX. You still believe in all that good stuff, don't you; our last Passionate Pilgrim. I'll tell something, Benito; if anyone can save pro bono from the barbarians, it's you.

BEN. "If?"

MAX. *Big* big if.

BEN. *(fighting the loss)* You're a shitty lawyer, a shitty friend, I hope you die a slow death alone in a motel room, now give me back my fucking tee-shirt.

MAX. *(with a grin)* I'll miss you, too.

(MAX offers his hand. Suddenly it's an embrace.
Enter JOBETH TRAUBE and ABE EINHORN, patriarch of D&R, a courtly, bemused-seeming elder with a sporadic nervous blink. JO, petite, low-key and stylish, has a wit as caustic as her smile is winning.)

MAX. *(hailing their arrival)* Mr. Einhorn... !

ABE. The media gentlemen are clamoring for you two heroes. I brought your beautiful wife to entice you downstairs.

JOBETH. *(to BENNETT)* The anchor from Channel 6 tried to pick me up, darling. If you're not careful ...

BEN. *(curtly)* Sorry, let's go. *(passing ABE as he exits)* Abe, may I have a word with you?

(He hurries out. ABE nods to JO, then slips out.)

JOBETH. What's going on, Max?

MAX. You look stunning.

JOBETH. Tell Bennett, maybe he'll notice — So do I get to hear what kept you up here so long? Good, bad, indifferent?

MAX. Less than a plane crash, more than a cough.

JOBETH. Would you accept that answer in court?

MAX. You're a classy number, Jo. I hope that blockhead appreciates what he's got.

(ABE re-enters, urging MAX down.)

JOBETH. *(not seeing ABE)* Lawyers only appreciate what *other* lawyers have, you know that.

ABE. Are we ready? *(JOBETH exits past ABE)* You couldn't wait till after his vacation to tell him?

MAX. He'll be fine.

ABE. And best of all, it's not your problem any more. Is it. *(MAX starts to reply, then thinks better of it and exits. ABE looks around the room, shaking his head slowly as he finds a TV remote balanced across two beer bottles.)* Good Lord, I hope the firm isn't paying for this mess.

(He flips on the TV and stands in its flickering light, watching as the lights fade slowly.)

TV. ... more on the Governor's dramatic resignation in a moment, now back to Chuck Kimball live from the Sands Radisson Hotel in downtown Mesa where lawyers from Donne & Russo are celebrating a remarkable victory, Chuck we know the Governor finally admitted voter fraud in Arroyo country, but do you think his racial slurs against

Native Americans helped turned the tide against him, or is his downfall due in large part to unrelenting legal work by Donne and Russo —

Scene 2 / Wilderness Campsite

(A bright orange tent is partly visible with a neat stack of firewood beside it. A ring of stones downstage defines a campfire site.
JOBETH, dressed for camping, aims a camcorder in our direction, slightly downhill.)

JOBETH. *(calling)* KYLE! STAY OFF THAT BOULDER, YOU'LL FALL!!! *KYLE! (beat)* THANK YOU, SWEETIE. STACY, PLEASE STAY UPSTREAM, IT'S TOO DEEP THERE. *(She sees BENNETT enter from the woods, absorbed in a paperback book, and turns the camcorder on him. He looks up with a cursory wave, then returns to his book. JOBETH lowers the camera.)* Why don't you make a fire, darling. I'll roast some wieners for lunch.
BEN. *(not looking up)* Sounds good —
JOBETH. You might read at night when the kids are asleep.
BEN. — almost done —
JOBETH. Let me introduce you to three wonderful people *(suddenly scratching her ankle)*; over here, being eaten alive by carriers of Rocky Mountain spotted fever — *Your Wife*!
BEN. *(edgy)* This is the only time I get to read for pleasure.
JOBETH. It's the only time we get to see you for any reason at all.
BEN. *(truce, tense, setting down the book)* I'll make a fire.
JOBETH. *(casually glancing at the book)* "Best American Essays of 1991." For pleasure!?

(BENNETT spots KYLE down the hill.)

BEN. *(calls)* HEY, BUDDY, LET'S SEE YOU DIVE!
JOBETH. NO!!! *(to BENNETT)* You *know* he can't swim. *(calls out)* KYLE, GET OFF THAT BOULDER, RIGHT NOW!

BEN. He's eight years old, for god sake. You know how I learned to swim?

JOBETH. Your father pushed you off a dock. He was a Marine. You're a lawyer. We call this evolution.

BEN. You'll make him afraid to take chances.

JOBETH. He's terrified of water. He's showing off to get your attention because there's no other way. *(A look. BENNETT fixes a fire. Relenting, JO kneels behind BENNETT and massages his back.)* Kyle told his class, "my dad's not a corpulent lawyer, he's an alligator and he eats other alligators in court. He meant you're a litigator, not corporate. I thought it was cute.

BEN. *(relishing the massage)* A little to the right. Yeah, *there*!

JOBETH. Your back feels like the World Encyclopedia of Knots

BEN. *(suddenly)* What if I quit D&R? Joined a smaller practice, something that left me time for a life.

JOBETH. This always happens when you unwind after a big case; self-doubts, moral crises, "Wither Me?!"

BEN. It's on my mind, Beth. If you don't want to hear it, fine, but please don't joke it away like it's some cuddly quirk of mine to question how much of my life I waste helping idiots with too much money make trouble for each other.

JOBETH. A little bad to pay for the good; that's the tradeoff.

BEN. Max was smart. He got out before everything — *(stops)* What if a few of us broke off to form a new firm, just trial work, like the early days, pure litigation. Less pay, but enough to get by? What would you say?

JOBETH. *(with control)* As in how would I like to trade the four bedroom Ranchero in Painted Valley for a rent controlled apartment in downtown Mesa? Maybe put an inflatable pool on the roof and move the kids from accelerated education to a public school, English a second language, crack on sale in the lunchroom? Well, darling, you're my husband, and your peace of mind is my deepest desire. That's the grown up answer. How do I *really* feel? - *(SCREAMS!)*

KYLE. *(off)* Mommy...!

JOBETH. IT'S OKAY, DARLING, MOMMY FOUND A MOUSE IN HER CANTEEN. *(Both smile)* That's better. Sweetie, I know you're upset about Max leaving —

BEN. *(jumps up)* This is not about Max. It's about twenty years building a firm you're proud of, and just when it feels solid, when you can finally relax, pick and chose cases, write a book maybe ... everything starts to slip and slide under your feet and the man who was supposed to keep the firm together, your best friend for god sake — okay, so it *is* about Max, big deal.

JOBETH. When the firm needed him, he walked away. Max was a coward. I've lost all respect for him.

BEN. *(he looks at her a moment, then decides to confide)* There's only one way it makes sense to stay at D&R.

JOBETH. You'll have to become Managing Partner.

BEN. *(appreciating her savvy)* Who've you been talking to?

JOBETH. Del's term is six more months. Not much time to campaign.

BEN. The litigators are with me. But the corporate section, I need their votes. Neat trick, after the hours I spent on the Governor! *(beat)* I have to make them trust me. They think I'm arrogant... aloof -

JOBETH. Money-money-money. Earn-earn-earn.

BEN. Exactly. Prove I speak their language. Get down in the trenches and make rain. And no pro bono. Nada. Zip. Fucking Max!

JOBETH. You're ten times the lawyer he was, everyone knows it.

BEN. We'd never see each other. Five years. Twenty-four hours a day. Seven days a week.

JOBETH. I don't like it either, darling. But you've given your life to the firm, you have to protect it.

BEN. I could lose.

JOBETH. You never do.

BEN. *(admiring)* Jobeth.

JOBETH. *(joking)* "Perfect Wife."

BEN. Okay. I'm going to go for it, Managing Partner of Donne & Russo. Amen, fingers crossed and hallelujah!

JOBETH. The other thing we do after a big case — we fight, then we kiss and stuff ... *(They kiss. It feels unfamiliar. Standing)* I aired the sleeping bags.

BEN. *(wary)* What about the kids? What about lunch?

JOBETH. The kids are playing. Lunch is hot weenies.

BEN. *(still hesitant)* Are you sure? You've been sort of cool on

all that lately ...
 JOBETH. Must we discuss it!
 BEN. There's no obligation is all I meant.
 JOBETH. *(desperate)* Just hold me, Bennett ... please. *(he embraces her; her head is on his shoulder:)* People envy us, you know. You don't notice those things, but it's important to me that you're respected and admired and good at what you do. I'm so proud of the life we've made. Why aren't you? *(suddenly upset)* What more could you want?
 BEN. Shhh. We have an incredibly good life. *(beat)* It's just so fucking expensive.

(Both chuckle. JOBETH is looking offstage.)

 JOBETH. I see four little eyeballs staring at us. *(she calls out)* WE'RE COMPARING HEIGHTS. DADDY'S TALLER TODAY.

(JOBETH lifts her tank top playfully.)

 BEN. Okay — lunch afterwards. What's gotten into you?
 JOBETH. Where's Kyle? *(calls)* STACY, WHERE'S YOUR BROTHER?!
 BEN. He's fine; look, climbing the boulder.
 JOBETH. KYLE, NO ... GET DOWN —
 BEN. *(calls out)* DIVE, KIDDO!!!
 JOBETH. *(hysterical)* He can't swim, Bennett, do something!

(Both stop and watch, utterly still.)

 BEN. *(suddenly points)* There! See, like a dolphin.
 JOBETH. If he'd hurt himself —
 BEN. He wants to jump, let him jump, damn it. *(beat)* Sorry. *(starting towards her)* You were saying?
 JOBETH. I think we missed the moment. *(beat)* What else is new?

(Lights fade.)

Scene 3 / Bennett's Office — Donne & Russo

(A Spartan office, walnut desk, computer station and little else. Beyond the picture window arid mountains outline a distant horizon.
BENNETT is catching up after his vacation when DEL GREGORIAN leans in.)

DEL. Got a minute?
BEN. Mr. G! What brings you down to us peons on 27?
DEL. I need your help.
BEN. What you need is a little R&R; fresh mountain air, the great outdoors ...
DEL. Go ahead, rub it in —
BEN. Coffee?
DEL. Look. *(hands him a computer tearout)* Some Young Turks in your section sent this e-mail yesterday.
BEN. "All first year associates in the Corporate Section are required to have a physical exam next Friday. They will continue at D&R only if they prove to be alive. The Shadow."

(BENNETT laughs ...)

DEL. This kind of disrespect crosses the line, Bennett ...
BEN. And what about corporate boycotting our victory?
DEL. That was — regrettable. We have to pull together. Speak to your guys. Tell them to use better judgement.
BEN. Leave it alone, Del. Corporate and litigation are always throwing sticks and stones. They're letting off steam, no big deal.

(DEL looks at BENNETT for a moment, wavers.)

DEL. *(slumps)* I had it all planned ... after Max took over, I'd apply for a year off. Travel abroad. Maybe meet someone; nice traditional type.

(He laughs at the absurdity of it.)

BEN. *(watching DEL)* When's your custody hearing?
DEL. *(shrugs)* We used to have a drink now and then, what happened there?
BEN. My door's always open.

(Enter CHRISTINE MARTEL, late 20s, blond hair, cloths trim and efficient, her gaze disconcertingly direct.)

CHRIS. Mr. Traube? I'm sorry, no one's at the desk out there, I was walking by and saw your name on the ... *(looks)* am I interrupting?
DEL. Not many of the old gang left. We have to set an example.
BEN. *(watching CHRISTINE)* We'll grab a drink after work. Okay?
CHRIS. I'm Christine Martel, LivEarth (as in "Live Earth") Coalition. I have no appointment.
DEL. *(sensing new energy)* Give my regards to your beautiful wife and two children. How does the song go? "Don't it always seem/ that you don't know what you have/and then it's gone ... tore down the parking lot, and put up a skyscraper... something, something." *(catching himself:)* Excuse me.

(DEL goes. CHRISTINE raises her eyebrow.)

BEN. *(explaining)* Our Managing Partner.
CHRIS. *(immediately:)* Del Gregorian, formerly litigation, moved to contract law. Major client, Laird Sutter Mining.
BEN. You have a thumbnail on everyone here, Ms. Martel? What's my file say — classic Donne & Russo type, funky off-the-wall manner meets state of the art technique?
CHRIS. Sorry, was I obnoxious? I never expected face time with *the* Bennett Traube. Nerves.
BEN. All right, rewind; you're with LivEarth?
CHRIS. Staff counsel.
BEN. Where's Clayton?

BUYING TIME 21

CHRIS. Washington; Bureau of Land Management. An offer he couldn't refuse. The old story.

BEN. Aren't you a little young to be so cynical?

CHRIS. I'm a little old to be patronized.

(BENNETT appraises her a moment.)

BEN. *(into intercom:)* Rita, two coffees.

CHRIS. I don't drink coffee.

BEN. They're for me, I like the second one cold. *(checking his watch)* Talk.

CHRIS. *(off balance)* Does the Tuintu Forest mean anything to you? Reinhardt Paper Industries?

BEN. Let me guess. They want to cut some trees?

CHRIS. Fifteen thousand acres to be exact. Old growth Ponderosa Pine. One of the last stands on earth.

BEN. Well, that's what they do.

CHRIS. And what I do is stop them.

BEN. I'm listening.

CHRIS. You know a bird called the Grayhawk?

BEN. *(seeing the strategy)* Endangered species ...

CHRIS. There's a brand new study that shows females stop laying eggs if their habitat shrinks. Less trees, less eggs, end of Grayhawk. Okay; the Tuintu is their last major habitat so if I argue that logging threatens their survival —

BEN. — Miss Martel —

CHRIS. — One more thing —

BEN. — Slow down. The Tuintu's a National Forest. Reinhardt can't touch a single pine cone without an Environmental Impact Statement, that'll take at least six months to move through the system, don't rush and make careless mistakes ...

CHRIS. Reinhardt started cutting a trail at 9:30 this morning.

BEN. On Tuintu land?

CHRIS. The road crew drove humongous yellow bulldozers right down I-9, like they couldn't care less who knows.

BEN. You *saw* this?

CHRIS. Once there's a road in, it's all over; campers, hunters, RVs; they'll pollute, scare off wildlife, start fires —

BEN. Stop them. File an injunction.

CHRIS. Will you help?

BEN. Ah. Sorry. LivEarth isn't my client.

CHRIS. We had Max Lasker. He's gone.

BEN. Only the Managing Partner can reassign work.

CHRIS. Make a request.

BEN. That would look suspicious, me chasing a routine matter.

CHRIS. *Routine*?! Saving fifteen thousand acres of first growth Ponderosa pine from a company involved in violations of NEPA and the possible extinction of a species?

BEN. *(ignoring the outburst)* I assure you that whoever we assign the case will do a first rate job.

CHRIS. Carter VanZant?

BEN. *(laughs) VanZant*?! *(calm)* Fine lawyer. Smart as hell —

CHRIS. A second year associate in real estate? He's never faced a judge, he knows none of the applicable law —

BEN. We encourage beginners to try all areas of practice. It gives them — depth.

CHRIS. In other words why waste your big guns on a nonpaying client like LivEarth?

BEN. Ms. Martel, every case feels like life or death when you're starting out. You don't want to screw up, I understand; it's a big deal replacing Clayton, but —

CHRIS. I'm not. I'm just filling in till they find someone. Jesus, they're so fucking disorganized. I swear, if the planet depends on people like them, say a prayer!

BEN. Don't personalize the law. You'll burn out.

CHRIS. Would you supervise VanZant? Just peek over his shoulder now and then — ?

BEN. *(pause)* Have you been to The Wells? It's a legal landmark. *(beat)* Every great litigator in town used to drink there before they moved the courthouse. *(beat)* Interested?

CHRIS. *(pause)* Wedding rings make me nervous.

BEN. Yes. Sorry. Look, if I could help you. But a case like this — for me right now, internally — never mind the *reasons* ... In two-three years it'll be a different story.

CHRIS. In two years there won't be a Tuintu Forest —

BEN. *(irritated)* Everyone has an agenda, Miss Martel, what's yours? LivEarth isn't wild to take on a big bad lumber company like Reinhardt, but if you get me on board you'll earn Brownie Points, maybe a full time job?

CHRIS. Are you always like this when a woman turns you down?

(Pause. BENNETT explodes with laughter.)

BEN. May I ask you something?
CHRIS. *(answer)* If you weren't married, yes, I'd have a drink.
BEN. That wasn't my question. But thank you.

(CARTER enters, irritated, holding a card.)

CARTER. These damn security cards keep jamming the elevator, that's the third time I've been trapped between floors, and with my claustrophobia — !

BEN. Christine Martel, this is Carter VanZant.

CARTER. *(seeing her)* Why, Miss Martel! What luck; twice in one day!

BEN. You've met?

CARTER. We enjoyed a working breakfast. As least, *I* enjoyed it.

BEN. Miss Martel wanted background on the Grayhawk.

CHRIS. *(direct)* No. I asked Mr. Traube to keep an eye on your work. No offense.

CARTER. *(beat)* No need to go behind my back, Miss Martel. I'm here to make the same request.

CHRIS. *(embarrassed)* I apologize. Dinner tonight's on *me*.

CARTER. In that case, you're forgiven. May we count on your help, Mr. Traube?

BEN. (carefully) If it goes beyond a routine action; if things get tricky — No promises. And keep my name out of it.

CARTER. Who's name? *(then, to CHRIS)* 8:15 at the cocktail lounge?

(CARTER smiles at BENNETT and waves goodbye with an attitude of

playful conspiracy.)

BEN. Yeah, bye Carter. *(CARTER leaves; mildly sarcastic:)* *Working* dinner?
CHRIS. I'm sorry for being — whatever. When things matter to me, I tend to go a little hyper — so I'm told.
BEN. Don't apologize. It's a good thing that you care about — it's good to care.
CHRIS. *(smiling)* What *was* your question? The one that wasn't about a drink?
BEN. Clayton's job, what's the salary?
CHRIS. Not enough to keep your Beemer in gas — if you're pondering a move down.
BEN. I drive a Ford, Ms. Martel.
CHRIS. Who's that supposed to fool, besides yourself?

(She rises.)

BEN. *(with edge)* I could put in a word for you. Is the reason I asked.
CHRIS. And I was teasing, Mr. Traube. Lighten up.

(CHRIS offers him her card, then goes. He watches where she left, then punches his intercom.)

BEN. Rita, go through Max's files, bring me anything you can find on Grayhawk. *(He releases the button, then has a further thought.)* Rita, about Grayhawk ... don't use my name. You're a beautiful person.

(He releases the button and stares at the door again.)

Scene 4 / Del Gregorian's Office — Donne & Russo

(Like BENNETT's office, but two windows, messier. MARGOT, HAL and PETE read identical newspapers.)

HAL. "Reinhardt Lumber's callous disregard for the extinction of the Grayhawk is nothing less than *ecocide* ..."

PETE. "Eco-side?!"

HAL. Wait, it gets better; "— than ecocide, said Carter VanZant, "one of Donne & Russo's most outspoken young *litigators*!

PETE. *Litigator* ...?

MARGOT. Yeah, I noticed that —

HAL. "Continued VanZant, 'LivEarth vs. Reinhardt Lumber could very well prove to be *the* environmental case of the 90s."

PETE. Why not the *century*? The history of mankind?!

HAL. I'm reminded of the mosquito floating down the river on his back with a hard-on yelling "Open the drawbridge, I'm coming through."

(BENNETT enters reading the same newspaper.)

MARGOT. Bennett, welcome to the coven.

BEN. *(looks around)* Where's VanZant?

PETE. Hiding under a rock if he has any sense.

BEN. Carter's one of your gang, Pete, you better deal with him before Del goes ballistic.

PETE. *(smirking)* I'm head of *corporate*. Carter's litigating, Hal's head of litigation; it's *his* problem now.

HAL. Let Margot take it. She's the tax division; a neutral third party.

MARGOT. Thanks for nothing. And forget about keeping Del out of orbit, it's already too late.

BEN. Why?

HAL. Did he not call us brave few to his office? Did we not expect to find VanZant? Q.E.D.; *(Dragnet theme)* Dum-de-dum-dum!

The Discipline Committee!!!

BEN. For this? *(waving the paper)* He'd never waste our time over a little pissant grandstanding like this ...

CARTER. *(entering)* My eggs were boiled perfectly this morning, I only hit two lights on Saddleback and the elevator didn't stick; it's a great day for Pisces.

PETE. If it isn't the overnight wonder of the courtroom himself! How's it feel to be litigating the most earth-shaking environmental case since the dawn of time?

CARTER. What can I say? The press inflated my credentials a tad.

BEN. Carter, you should know better than to fight a case through the press; it's low rent, it's stupid and it's very very dangerous.

CARTER. *(flip)* You guys get network time for the Governor and you begrudge me one bitty piece in the local rag?

PETE. It's not a joke, you stupid son of a bitch.

BEN. *(gentle warning)* Pete. *(to Carter)* This kind of posturing creates the impression that our firm favors one type of client over another. We're trying hard to correct a reputation for slight anti-corporate bias ...

PETE. "Slight" in the sense that sperm whales are *slightly* bigger than sardines.

CARTER. Did I violate a company rule?

PETE. It's not about rules, it's about common sense. *(to HAL)* Okay, okay, I'll take this one. *(to VanZANT)* You ruffled a lot of feathers today, my friend; big birds who lay big golden eggs. Hooray, you're litigating a case, Dorothy, but you're still in corporate and I'm your section head, so any more bright ideas, run 'em by me first. Got it?

DEL. *(enters, all efficiency)* All here? Good. *(into intercom)* Hold my calls; meeting. *(He holds out the newspaper.)* Mr. VanZant, explain this.

CARTER. Had I known I'd be so popular today, I'd have worn my Armani suit.

BEN. *(warning)* Carter!

DEL. *(to CARTER)* Max assigned this case to you, god knows why. He clearly saw talent where I see none, but in respect of his judgement I'll give you a chance to explain yourself before this matter goes on your record.

BEN. Del, this doesn't fall under Discipline. You can't mess up the guy's future over a small lapse of judgement.

DEL. Fine. You obviously know how to handle it, why don't *you* deal with Sutter breathing down your neck all morning, "What's with the *Mesa Herald*, are you guys biting the hand that feeds you?" You want to field his calls, you want to catch his flack?

HAL. *(to CARTER)* Laird Sutter's the original Client From Hell.

PETE. We like his money though, don't we, Harold?

CARTER. I attacked Reinhardt, Reinhardt is *lumber*; Sutter is *mining*. What's the connection?

MARGOT. Out here it's all one animal; lumber, mining, oil, ranchers; the Extractive Mafia, we call 'em. They exploit public lands, pay off lawmakers, and deal harshly with anyone who gets in their way.

HAL. Only don't repeat that in a room full of strangers wearing string ties, if you get my meaning.

CARTER. *(beat)* That's outrageous! Sutter's harassing us because his buddy Reinhardt asked him to? Do I smell a Nasty?

BEN. Very nasty.

CARTER. May I pursue it?

MARGOT. *(half-amused)* He doesn't understand.

DEL. I hereby convene the Discipline Committee to decide appropriate action ... Margot, take notes ...

MARGOT. I'm a lawyer, not a secretary.

BEN. *(uneasy)* Del, give it a rest. Please.

DEL. *(to CARTER)* Continue, VanZant. We're listening.

CARTER. What happened to all the stirring tales of D&R's unorthodox style; how your innovative lawyering turned routine cases into landmark law and so on. I even took less pay for the chance to work in such a bold legal environment. Now the first time I try something offbeat, I'm hauled in front of the highest Poo-Bahs in the firm for discipline?!

BEN. Just a friendly warning; avoid the press ...

PETE. Now lets all go back to our little work stations and churn the economy, shall we?

CARTER. May I finish?

DEL. Please. I want it in the record.

CARTER. I tried an injunction. Did it stop Reinhardt? No. So what do you use on a man when he acts above the law? The only thing more powerful; media. My article caught his road crew with their panties down round their muddy little boots, by noon their work site was swarming with press and had to shut down. Thus buying me time to prepare a case. Now if in pursuit of my client's interests, I happen to stir mud within the waters of D&R, I'd have to say that's the firm's problem, not mine.

PETE. *(springs up)* Some of us weren't born with rich daddies, VanZant. If any of my guys lose so much as one thin dime of income over your shenanigans, I will personally mop all five floors of Donne & Russo with that supercilious smile of yours.

(PETE barges out.)

MARGOT. *(wryly)* Should it go in the minutes that Mr. Water left?

LANE. *(leaning in)* Mr. Einhorn's on his way. Have a nice day.

(He exits quickly.)

DEL. Meeting adjourned. Bennett, stay here, would you? Van-Zant, you, too. Everyone else can go —

MARGOT. *(sarcastic)* Don't we need a motion to adjourn — ?

DEL. That's enough, Margot.

(Enter ABE EINHORN. He takes in the room, then circles the group with a benign smile.)

ABE. I was watching a rerun of L.A. Law the other night, did anyone happen to catch it?

CARTER. Is that the one where —

ABE. — Perhaps it dates me, but they do seem to exaggerate the amount of fornication that goes on in a law office. Not that I'm against productivity. *(beat)* You're VanZant?

CARTER. Yes, sir.

ABE. May I suggest more time at the desk, and less with the press.

CARTER. *(calm)* Whatever serves my client. Sir.

(ABE fully notes CARTER's impudence, and gives him a patient pat on the sleeve.)

ABE. That's right, you're from money. *(turns abruptly to DEL)* So our old friend Sutter's been in touch.

DEL. With friends like that!

ABE. *(chuckles)* Laird Sutter is Old West; he takes things to heart. A little personal attention is all he needs. You. VanZant. Bennett, maybe you could attend ... with your wives and/or current companions.

BEN. Attend what?

ABE. An informal dinner, his place. Thursday. Regrettably, I'm called to Washington on business.

DEL. What's the object? Do we offer something; a gesture, an apology?

ABE. Your presence itself is the gesture. That our most distinguished partners would grace his table shows we care. *(a grin of mischief)* Sutter's home is worth a visit. I call particular attention to the stuffed grizzly in his hallway. And his wife's idea of fashion is ... memorable. *(starts out, turns back)* He'll be delighted to hear that you accept.

(ABE leaves. A moment passes.)

HAL. Good luck, warriors. Sounds like heaps o' fun.

MARGOT. Do we like this idea?

BEN. Why not? Show the flag, pump a little sunshine. The personal touch.

(As PETE and HAL leave:)

DEL. *(to CARTER)* Thursday. Best behavior. I'll be watching you, VanZant. *(CARTER is about to object, but MARGOT pushes him out the door hissing quietly "Just keep moving.")* I wanted that smart-ass scared, you undercut me, that's no good —

(He stops.)

BEN. Get a grip, Del. Come on, let's blow this pop stand, grab a brew at The Wells —

DEL. Don't humor me, Bennett. This firm could go belly up during my reign.

BEN. Del; Kings reign; Managing Partners "serve." And no one's going belly up.

DEL. Look out there *(the window)*; Clavert & Peele hasn't paid a partner in five months. Recession, hell, it's a wasteland, no one has money for law these days, and Sutter knows it. He'll bleed us dry.

BEN. Knock a few bucks off his next bill. Didn't he bitch us out over a thirty dollar Xerox fee on a half million dollar invoice; the man's defective.

DEL. This is bigger than Sutter. It's payback time ...

BEN. What!?

DEL. We let Corporate run wild, talk us into this high rise to impress their clients. Have you seen the overhead, how did we let it happen?

BEN. *(playing along)* Grow or die, wasn't that the party line?

DEL. It was greed. We had the whole nine yards and wanted more; money in one hand, pro bono in the other. But the two don't mix. This is the reckoning; "And he shall bring every work into judgement, whether it be good, or whether it be evil." Do you know Ecclesiastes?

BEN. I thought you quit the ministry for law school.

DEL. *(eerily jaunty)* Dierdre sold the house. In this market! I'm wiped out. She wants the kids, too. No visiting rights. *(vacant)* She used to have these nightmares - I'd hold her all night long.

(BENNETT waits for the moment to pass.)

BEN. I'm sorry, Del.

DEL. *(dismissive)* To hell with it, personal stuff.

BEN. I could keep an eye on VanZant.

DEL. Stay well out of it.

BEN. No one has to know.

DEL. The way lawyers gossip? Hell, we're worse than hairdressers; if I had a heart attack right this minute every attorney in town would know before I hit the floor.

BEN. Carter's not qualified if this thing gets tricky.

DEL. *(cold)* Chinese Wall, Bennett. *(sits at his desk and works)* You here, Grayhawk there.

BEN. What's the problem?

DEL. As Managing Partner, I take full responsibility.

BEN. Are you trying to bury this case in the minor league?

DEL. Your time is too valuable to waste on routine business.

BEN. And with no one big attached, you can offer it to Sutter as a sacrificial lamb?

DEL. I have lots of people to keep happy, Bennett. *(smiles)* Go make some money. *(beat)* Hey, we're on the same team, remember? Lunch tomorrow? Bring the vacation pix; show me how it looks to be relaxed.

(BENNETT watches DEL ignoring him as he returns to his work. Lights fade.)

Scene 5 / Christine's Apartment — Downtown Mesa

(A 1930s adobe bungalow. Southwest Native-American craftwork in a Spartan decor. An overhead fan.

Legal papers are scattered everywhere. A stereo plays dreamy "environmental" music.

CHRISTINE, in khaki shorts and net tank top — it's a hot evening, leads BENNETT in. He's in a rumpled jacket and oxford shirt. He looks tired.)

CHRIS. You were driving by, my light was on, it's 10 PM — ?

BEN. *(raising his briefcase in explanation)* An old case of mine, Spotted Owl vs. Oregon Timber. I won, slam dunk. You can plug in Grayhawk and everything tracks.

CHRIS. A Greek bearing gifts. Does this mean bad news? Let me guess, you won't supervise?

BEN. *(pause)* Carter blew it. His interview made Grayhawk glow in the dark. The bad guys'll be watching it like Monday Night Football.

CHRIS. *(Q.E.D.)* If you'd been counseling us —

BEN. Are you and Carter an item? Is he trying to impress you?

CHRIS. He's trying to get your firm's attention. *And* stop the road. Looks like he hit a double bull's eye.

BEN. He hit a hornet's nest, and my firm's going to get stung.

CHRIS. Could you be more specific?

BEN. No.

CHRIS. *(pause)* Would bad red wine make a difference? Or slightly better scotch?

BEN. No. Thank you. *(carefully)* Look, Ms. Martel, there's a rift within D&R of long standing — and of a nature which might behoove a client like LivEarth to seek alternate counsel.

CHRIS. Max took this case five months ago. Now suddenly we're poison because of one little item in the newspaper?

BEN. "Little?!" Centerfold feature; child clutching dead Grayhawk? Reinhardt headquarters with skull and crossbones superimposed — ?

CHRIS. *(interrupting)* Are you dropping us?

BEN. *(utterly miserable)* That drink — is it still available?

CHRIS. No; I mean, first tell me what's so urgent it takes a visit at 10 PM?

BEN. *(beat)* Our firm has a bylaw about pro bono —

CHRIS. Rule 7: "Partners may use 20% of their billable hours for public interest work with full pay and bonus entitlement."

BEN. That's right, you know everything about us, don't you?

CHRIS. It's a legend in the legal world; rob from corporate to fight for the meek.

BEN. This attitude thing, is it to prove you're hip and worldly

wise, cause I find it incredibly irritating.
 CHRIS. I'm just protecting myself.
 BEN. From what?
 CHRIS. Whatever you're having so much trouble telling me; it feels ominous.
 BEN. Well guess what, this is hard for me, too ... trying to explain why my firm, a firm I'm very proud of — might be at a moment where we're compelled to act in a way — I'm not very proud of.
 CHRIS. Why should I consider alternate counsel, Mr. Traube?
 BEN. Because ... this is a bad time for idealists. We have to pick our battles with care.
 CHRIS. *(pointed)* Why should I consider alternate counsel?
 BEN. We may be compelled to please certain clients at the expense of others. I really can't say any more. *(beat)* I shouldn't even be here, I better go.
 CHRIS. Scotch, was it? *(She pours. BENNETT steals a glance at his watch; seeing this:)* You have one of those watches that tells you the next move?
 BEN. Without ice. *(beat)* You live alone? Witty repartee.
 CHRIS. *(pouring his drink)* I'm *not* an idealist, Mr. Traube. I need access, not protection.
 BEN. Bennett. Please.
 CHRIS. I want Reinhardt for personal reasons. Irrational, even. Which is usually why we do things, don't you think?
 BEN. Odd view for a lawyer.
 CHRIS. To beat Reinhardt you need something crazy driving you; as crazy as whatever's driving him; arrogance, presumption, greed — I don't know, what is it that lets one man destroy irreplaceable things in the world then sleep through the night? We'll fight by the rules, of course; Courtroom, judge, all that civilized stuff. But just under the skin it's a state of nature, and the maddest blood always wins — always.
 BEN. Is that your legal theory for the case?
 CHRIS. I had this uncle, Granger — a park ranger he was ...
 BEN. Granger the Ranger?
 CHRIS. *(smiles acknowledgement)* He'd go on these benders and pass out for days. I rode his horse into the woods, and I'd wear a

blindfold. It was a game; no, a challenge. I had to wind up somewhere I wouldn't recognize when I took the blindfold off, then let my horse go and find my way home, only a knife and matches allowed. And the trick was to never let fear in. One time I was out five days. I fell asleep thinking, "Tonight I'll die , and animals will eat me. I'll vanish without trace." *(smiles at herself)* I was a dramatic child.

BEN. How'd you get home?

CHRIS. You're missing the point. I'm talking about fear, how you master it. How I learned not to be afraid, ever. That forest became mine in he end; my wild place.

BEN. *(beat)* Is there some reason you're telling me this?

CHRIS. Reinhardt cut it down years ago. Ranger lost his job, drank himself to death. End of story.

BEN. So this is revenge.

CHRIS. *(focussed)* The Tuintu's a lot like that forest. Ponderosa Pine; a very powerful tree. Reinhardt wants to cut down another wild place like the one where I was happy once. So, I'm going to destroy him.

BEN. Well. *(what can he say)* Good luck.

CHRIS. Are you not listening, or don't you take me seriously.

BEN. *(suddenly)* I came here to make love.

CHRIS. Oh.

(CARLOS, mid-20s, enters through the archway behind, his shirt open to show nipple rings. Seeing BENNETT, he kisses CHRISTINE on the lips.)

CARLOS. Almost done here? I lust for guacamole.

CHRIS. I'll meet you for dessert; *later*. *(with meaning)* This is Bennett.

CARLOS. *(offering his hand)* "Carlos."

(They shake. CARLOS leaves.)

BEN. *(embarrassed now)* I'm sorry. You have company.

CHRIS. He lives with me. *(then)* I mean, "here." The apartment.

BEN. *(not understanding)* Cozy.

CHRIS. *(sees that BENNETT misconstrued)* We're meeting Carter if you'd like to join us. It's their first date ...
BEN. Date? *(pause)* Carter and — *(the guy he just met!)*
CHRIS. D&R, ever on the cutting edge!
BEN. I had no idea.

(CHRISTINE giggles. Re-enter CARLOS.)

CARLOS. You mean Bennett, as in *Bennett*-Bennett?
CHRIS. *(fondly)* Later, you fool.
CARLOS. *(playful)* He doesn't look *that* old ....

(CARLOS exits. CHRIS is blushing a little.)

BEN. Ahah! *(teasing)* And exactly how old *do* I look?
CHRIS. *(blushing)* All right, the *exact* debate was: older married man with reputation makes pass. Should I go for it and become another notch on his belt, or do the right thing and spend years wondering what I missed? Carlos and I were planning further debate on this issue over dinner when the doorbell rang and — Guess Who?!
BEN. About my reputation...
CHRIS. What number would I be? Thirty? Forty?
BEN. A few days ago you said *no* to a drink.
CHRIS. I wasn't afraid then.
BEN. You have to be afraid?
CHRIS. I like something to get past. Seventy? Seventy-five? Am I warm?
BEN. I don't count. The truth is — you really want to know?
CHRIS. Yes. Talk while I make up my mind.
BEN. I used to promise myself, after every big case, if I won — which I usually do — I'd treat myself. A reward.
CHRIS. *(impressed)* That's great! What a *guy* thing! How many cases have you won? *(beat)* I can look it up.
BEN. I said "big" cases.
CHRIS. Like the Governor; am I the reward?
BEN. He was a very big case.
CHRIS. That works for me. *(He moves forward. Now they're*

close, but for a moment neither moves. Then suddenly they kiss, both of them intense and awkward. She stops, then slips free to find her drink, playing for time.) Do you really keep count?

BEN. *(beat)* No.

CHRIS. Some fantasy.

BEN. It's a thing Max used to do, after every case. I never understood that. He loves his wife. I don't play around.

CHRIS. And that invitation to the Wells?

BEN. It's not a habit, Chris.

CHRIS. I thought my professional manner kept that sort of thing at a distance. No one ever came out of left field like that.

BEN. *(meaning to end it)* You have a good chance with Grayhawk. I wish I could help.

(He starts to go, then turns back and approaches her. She doesn't move. They kiss. It begins to catch fire. CHRISTINE draws back.)

CHRIS. *(beat)* Bennett, let's say good night. I'm sorry, this isn't something I can do right now.

BEN. *(helping her)* "Chinese Wall?" *(explains)* An expression at work; Law *here*, feelings *there*.

CHRIS. Yes. Chinese Wall. Thank you for the documents.

BEN. You're welcome.

(But it's not over. He moves towards her.)

CHRIS. Please go before I change my mind.

(BENNETT nods, touches her face, then leaves.)

Scene 6 / Laird Sutter's Family Room

(The shadow of a stuffed Grizzly falls across the floor from the hallway. BECKY, LAIRD's wife, in a chair, takes occasional sips from a large glass, then returns to a stillness which makes her blend with the decor. She wardrobe is heavy on gold and leopard skin, and she looks between 30 and 60 years of age.
LAIRD and DEL enter under the arch eating off paper plates. LAIRD wears silver snakeskin boots, suit and Stetson. His voice booms and his manner is overbearing, but he has a certain brutish charm. He turns back and takes aim at:)

LAIRD. *(to DEL, as guide)* There's Grizz! You don't know fear till you've seen them red eyes burning down on you full of blood and hallelujah! *(aiming a finger at grizz)* Pow! *(to DEL)* I'll have to take you hunting one day.

DEL. *(faux bonhomie)* I'd like that.

LAIRD. *(guffaws)* Of course you would. And where might I ask is your good lady wife tonight, Mr. Gregorian?

DEL. School Committee. She sends regrets.

LAIRD. Of course she does.

(Enter BENNETT and JOBETH with food on paper plates. JO is controlling the giggles.)

JOBETH. We were just admiring your choice of architecture — A daring statement. For the Rockies.

LAIRD. Copied brick by brick from a castle in Scotland built by Lord Royston Sutter, a great-grand-something of mine, fifth Earl of sheepshit and who gives a damn, right?! *(laughs)* May I show you the ballroom, Mrs. Traube. If your husband will trust me alone with his beautiful lady wife.

BEN. *(gracious)* I'll keep an eye on the time.

LAIRD. Of course you will! *(laughs)*

(Enter CARTER and TROY, Sutter, Jr., a handsome bovine lad of 20.

Both eat from paper plates.)

TROY. Cairo won't answer her door, Dad. She's upstairs sulking.
LAIRD. Tell her to hustle that skinny butt-bone of hers down here PDQ or I'll flush every credit card she owns down the toilet.
TROY. Yes, sir. *(to others)* Pardon me ...

(As TROY leaves, CARTER holds his paper plate.)

LAIRD. Troy has his mind set on law school. I hope you'll forgive a doting father for inviting you masters of the trade up here to advise him?

(DEL looks at BENNETT. Did he hear right?)

DEL. Excellent chili, Mr. Sutter.
JOBETH. What a fun idea, paper plates; a picnic indoors!
LAIRD. *(to JOBETH)* This way, Mrs. Traube, or may I call you — what was the name again?
JOBETH. *(exiting with LAIRD)* JoBeth —
LAIRD. *(escorting her off)* The ballroom seats five hundred, as you may have read in *Sunset Magazine*, allow me —

(He leads her off. DEL turns to BENNETT, trying to contain his excitement.)

DEL. D'you hear what he said? We're here to advise his kid!
BEN. *(smiles)* There may be more to it, Del.
DEL. Wouldn't that be something; we sweat bullets all week, it turns out he's just showing off for his son.

(BECKY issues a single gunshot of laughter —)

BECKY. HA! Believe that and I'll sell you Canada.

(DEL, BENNETT and CARTER are startled by her.)

BEN. Mrs. Sutter, I beg your pardon —

BECKY. — you didn't see me, I know.
DEL. *(sociably)* It must feel grand to be mistress of a setup like this.

(BECKY studies DEL for a moment.)

BECKY. "Grand" doesn't begin to capture what I feel.
TROY. *(re-entering)* Cairo won't listen to me, ma'm.
BECKY. Who the fuck cares about Cairo? Do you? *I* don't.
TROY. Dad wants her down.
BECKY. Your father wants everyone down, down and bleeding from the nostrils, and that, my big gorgeous Troyboy, is *his* problem.
LAIRD. *(re-enters with JOBETH)* I'm impressed with your wife's eye for color. Becky could use some help in the decor department. You two should have lunch. Becky doesn't get out much these days ...
DEL. *(long pause)* So Troy wants to be a lawyer?
LAIRD. Troy doesn't know *what* he wants. Isn't that what law school is for, people who don't know what they want to do when they grow up? And if they never figure it out, why they can just become lawyers.

(LAIRD chuckles. No one knows if his insults are provocations, or a matter of character.)

TROY. I applied to Harvard, Stanford and Tulane.
CARTER. Tulane's my neck of the woods. You'd find New Orleans very *welcoming*. A little something for every taste.

(He and TROY exchange the briefest look.)

BEN. Are we really here to advise your son, Mr. Sutter?
DEL. *(temporizing)* Harvard is *my* alma mater. I recommend it.
BECKY. What about artichokes with vinaigrette sauce, do you recommend them, too, as long as we're gonna talk about everything but the dead cow floating in the swimming pool.
LAIRD. *(a pause)* You'll have to pardon my wife. She gets these strange signals from a distant galaxy.

BECKY. *(extending her glass to TROY)* Top me up, sugar — to where it spills when your hand shakes.

(TROY moves to obey. LAIRD holds him in place.)

LAIRD. Mr. Traube, as a husband and father, I'm sure you'll appreciate the lengths a man will go to to provide for his family ...
JOBETH. *(pause)* My husband is speechless with appreciation. *(with a look both playful and urgent)* Aren't you, darling?
BEN. *(finally)* I had a good experience at Stanford.
TROY. I find myself leaning towards Tulane, myself.
LAIRD. *(deceptive charm)* Tell us what is it about Tulane that got you leaning in that particular direction, Troy.
TROY. They say it has an excellent faculty, sir.
LAIRD. They say that falling in love is wonderful, so what? Name this excellent faculty, what books of theirs have you read, which eminent alumni have you questioned in depth to get you leaning in their particular direction?
CARTER. *(protecting TROY)* Tulane is first rate academically —
LAIRD. I'm talking to my son. What do you know about Tulane, Troy Sutter?!
TROY. I mainly know —
LAIRD. You mainly know shit is what you mainly know, besides how to butter my butt till I'm pushing up daisies ... like its only the women around here waiting for me to keel over dead so they can start pissing away my hard earned money on booze and clothing and what not; automobiles! Now get your mother a gi-normous drink and take your sweet time.
BECKY. *(as TROY takes her glass)* Remember his weak heart, darling. He can't last much longer.

(TROY exits. CARTER moves to follow him.)

LAIRD. *(to CARTER)* Where are *you* going, Mr. VanZant?!
BECKY. It's show time!
LAIRD. I thought you might have something to tell me.
DEL. *(urging him on)* Carter —

CARTER. *(with great care)* The reporter quoted much of what I said out of context.

LAIRD. That's your best shot? After careful coaching by these masters of the trade? You see, I'm taking what you say now to be the official Donne & Russo posture on this newspaper business.

BEN. He speaks for himself, Mr. Sutter. We don't coach people for dinner parties, only trials.

JOBETH. *(attempting to avert a train wreck)* Where did you find that stunning material for the couch, Mrs. Sutter?

BECKY. Somewhere that sells lots of fabric. Pinkish building. Brain, brain, what's the name? A Jew owns it. Needless to say.

DEL. Carter, tell Mr. Sutter how that interview came about.

BECKY. If the plan was to grovel, kids, save your breath. Tonight my husband's in a mood for blood-and-entrails.

LAIRD. Damn shame when a woman loses all sense of dignity.

BECKY. The shame is underestimating your current wife as badly as you did the first four. Come on, lawyers, half the man's money is mine, now what's your offer?!

DEL. You see, Carter spoke to that reporter off the record —

CARTER. *(with attempted restraint)* Had I known I might offend another client of the firm — even a client with no direct interest in my case … I assure you I'd have …

DEL. *(to LAIRD)* Mr. VanZant is relatively new to D&R; to the west, in fact.

(LAIRD speaks to CARTER inches from his face.)

LAIRD. Are you familiar with work of Thucydides?

BECKY. Here we go. *(calls out)* TROY, WHERE'S MOMMY'S DRINK?

LAIRD. — the Greek historian. Am I the only one left who reads Greek and Latin? "An alliance can hold only as long as an attack on *one* party is viewed as an attack upon all."

BEN. Actually we're more familiar with the Italian Mario Puzo, who writes about Mafia beating up on people who won't do business their way. Now if your friend Reinhardt asked you as a personal favor to lean on us —

DEL. — Mr. Sutter, allow us to handle this internally. We'll resolve the problem to your complete satisfaction.
BECKY. How?!
BEN. Yes, Del, what does *that* mean?

(DEL is startled by BENNETT's interjection.)

LAIRD. I'm satisfied that Mr. Gregorian understands.
BEN. But *I* don't. What exactly do you want from us? A written apology? A retraction in the *Herald*? A break on your next billing?
BECKY. You're not in the ball park, Mr. Traube. You're barely in the parking lot.

(TROY re-enters and hands BECKY a huge drink. All eyes follow him. He smiles around.)

TROY. I've changed my mind. Medical school!

(With a roar of laughter, he soars from the room on a cocaine thermal.)

LAIRD. TROY! GOD DAMN IT, WHERE'S YOUR SISTER?
CARTER. *(turns to go)* I better see if he's all right ...
LAIRD. Don't you budge, VanZant.
CARTER. *Mister* VanZant to you. The *IVth*, to be exact. You know, I grew up thinking that just about every desirable human trait you could name was bred out of my family generations ago. But next to the Sutters, we weren't a bad outfit. Please take this moment to piss upon my more senior colleagues whilst I dry out briefly under the desert moon.

(He exits.)

BECKY. *(chuckles)* That boy has spunk.
JOBETH. *(with tact)* Perhaps we should leave Del and Mr. Sutter to work this out in private ...
BECKY. Who the hell invited Betty Boop?
LAIRD. Becky-May, you're a disgrace to womankind, now shut

your hideous mouth.

BEN. You may be a client, Mr. Sutter, but so is LivEarth. And since the two of you have no business in common, I'll ask you to butt out.

LAIRD. The same to you, Mr. Traube. As I understand it, Grayhawk is not your case.

BEN. Didn't you hear? I'm supervising.

DEL. *(to BEN)* Absolutely not. You have no authority —

BEN. I can submit a request —

DEL. — Denied.

BEN. — I'll do it off the clock —

DEL. Bennett, could we *please* talk about this tomorrow.

BEN. *(to DEL)* I don't know what you're up to, Mr. Sutter. Maybe you're pissed off that we nailed your friend the Governor; if he helped your interests around the state as much they say, I can certainly appreciate your anger. Or maybe you're just yanking our chain as a favor to your lumbering buddy Reinhardt, who knows —

JOBETH. — Darling —

BEN. — But either way, I don't give a shit, and please excuse the language, not to mention the hostility, I have this thing, probably genetic, try asking where your wife buys this glorious fabric of hers, the Jew owner, you know, maybe he can explain my hatred of bullies —

JOBETH. — Bennett —

BEN. — Grayhawk is a solid case which I can win fair and square, and guess what; there isn't one tiny fucking shred of a thing you can do about it, goodnight ...

LAIRD. *(grinning)* Nice try, Mr. Traube. But the thing with ole Grizz, if you don't score a clean hit with the first shot, why he'll just keep right on coming.

JOBETH. Bennett, for god sake, let's go.

BEN. *(beckoning)* Del ...

DEL. I'll be along.

BEN. *(choosing his words with care)* I think it would be advisable, for appearances sake, if we all left together.

LAIRD. Mr. Gregorian, as your client, I ask you to tarry a moment. *(DEL is torn between BENNETT/JOBETH, and the demand of SUTTER. BENNETT and JOBETH leave.)* I expected this evening to end on a different note.

(He approaches his wife and kisses her gently.)

DEL. You should have let me handle the matter quietly.
LAIRD. Sometimes it helps clarify a situation to get it out in the open, don't you find?
DEL. How can we settle this matter? What can we offer?
LAIRD. I'd never presume to meddle in the internal affairs of your company. You must do as you see fit. And when I am satisfied, I shall make it known.
DEL. I can't drop Grayhawk. Not with Bennett attached.
LAIRD. I thought Managing Partner was a position of particular power in your firm.
DEL. Bennett is one of our most respected and influential partners. If he made a fuss ... what you're asking could have devastating repercussions ...
LAIRD. I asked nothing. Let's be very clear on that point.
DEL. Our firm has a deep investment in cases like Grayhawk. You knew our reputation when you came to us.
LAIRD. And you knew mine. I tell you what we have here; we have a narrow bridge across a very deep canyon. And right in the middle of that bridge, we have two cars face to face with room for only one to pass. That's what we have here, Mr. Gregorian. Regards to your lovely wife. *(DEL start out, then turns to speak; cutting him off:)* Good night.

(DEL exits. LAIRD paces, agitated.)

BECKY. Some friends of ours are going to be a tad disappointed, hon.
LAIRD. Take your pills and get to bed, darlin'. I got a mess of work to do tonight. Love you to pieces. Sleep tight.

(BETTY starts to exit as LAIRD stands stock still, staring into his plans, calculating the strategy ahead.)

END OF ACT I

ACT II

Scene 1 / Partner's Lounge — Donne & Russo

(A long conference table with chairs. The room is posted with "NO SMOKING" signs. An American flag hangs in the corner.
Lights up on DEL, MARGOT, HAL and PETE speaking over each other loudly.)

MARGOT.	HAL.	PETE.	DEL.
Did Sutter demand; did he actually — Pete, okay, but — He's *your* client, Del, what's your gut on this thing?	What'd he actually say — get it in writing and we'll nail him to a cactus, if it ain't on paper, fuck him —	What's his exact position; do we know for a fact he wants Greyhawk or is this just us second guessing?	*(with growing heat)* All he said was — just a minute, Margot; Please, quiet, everyone. QUIET ...!!!

MARGOT. It's Panic City upstairs, how do we calm the troops?

DEL. Any talk of dropping Grayhawk is rumor and hearsay.

PETE. So why are my guys getting headhunter calls, "How's things at D&R, let's have lunch," why do we smell vulnerable overnight?

MARGOT. Forget the "why," Pete, everyone knows what's going on here — a classic Sutter disinformation campaign; rumors, gossip, a few calls round town and we look like a firm in trouble. The question is what's he after?

HAL. Maybe in a former life we ran a Nazi death camp. There must be a reason God punished us with a client like this.

MARGOT. Did Bennett really attack Sutter last night, or is that another rumor?

DEL. Just assure your sections everything is under control.

HAL. That makes *us*, *Chernobyl* and *Tiananmen Square*.

DEL. All we need is a gesture to show the firm is responsive to the specific needs of a client like Laird Sutter.

PETE. What gesture, Del? This is surreal. There's a ten ton gorilla sitting on the porch with a sign that says "Guess what I want?" and we're supposed to throw stuff out the door 'til he smiles?

DEL. Let me approach the problem from another angle.

MARGOT. This better be good, Delmore.

DEL. You all received the 3rd quarter revenue report last night. *(displays pages)* The overall performance of certain associates is clearly disappointing.

(BEN enters, looking around.)

BEN, Sorry … I was held up —

(He stops, sensing the tension.)

DEL. — In light of the recession, which shows no signs of an upturn in the near future, we can't for the moment afford the luxury of carrying unproductive associates. *(passes a list)* Here's a list of people I'd recommend we terminate.

HAL. Wild guess; is Carter VanZant on that list?

DEL. *(looks at the list)* Let me see —

MARGOT. Del, don't pretend to look …

PETE. You can't have VanZant. You want a burnt offering for Sutter, find someone else …

DEL. I'm proposing a more general weeding out process —

PETE. VanZant stays. He's a pissant, but he's *my* pissant, and he's been a good earner.

HAL. Fire a hundred associates, if VanZant is one of them everyone'll know who you're after, and why —

PETE. *(without enthusiasm)* How about this: reassign the case to someone in Hal's section, have them sit on it 'til LivEarth gets pissed off at the poor service and walks?

BEN. *(stepping in)* These impromptu strategy sessions make the guys upstairs nervous. Let's meet *outside* the building from now on, 'til this thing blows over. We can review Del's proposal individually, and discuss it over breakfast tomorrow, Taco Bell?

(All exchange looks, then rise to go.)

MARGOT. What if Sutter was unhappy with me, Del. Or *you*. How would we respond to his specific need — I find myself wondering.

PETE. If it's even half-true what you did to Sutter last night; forget inexcusable, forget the example it sets ... if any associate of mine provoked a client that way I'd march him in front of the Discipline Committee so damn fast his head would spin.

(He exits.)

HAL. *(to BEN)* Income is Pete's religion; you defiled his God.

(HAL, MARGOT and PETE leave ...)

DEL. *(in a rage)* Don't you ever dare break up a meeting of mine like that again. I'm still Managing Partner, in case it's escaped your notice ...

BEN. *(controlled)* You were shooting yourself in the foot, Del. Hey, it's me, Bennett; peace.

DEL. Peace? After last night? Okay, Sutter's difficult, but look what you started, and for what: LivEarth? A bunch of macrobiotic zombies in a storefront on Clifton?

BEN. You mean they don't have money, like Sutter. Is that how we're assigning preference, is this some new policy you forgot to tell us about ... ?

DEL. LivEarth isn't your client, Bennett. You went to war for people you don't represent —

BEN. — on my own time —

DEL. You provoked him. Deliberately. Why?

BEN. What can I say? I'm sorry, okay? I'm sorry you're caught in the middle. I threatened your client, I apologize. But telling him where to get off, no, no, I'd do it again. After last night, Jesus, Del, his contempt for us ... you could choke on it.

DEL. *(resolute)* This could have been handled quietly.

BEN. Like what? Drop Grayhawk in a closed vote of the steering committee? Sweep it under the carpet?

DEL. That's my job. I make the ugly stuff go away that one wants to look at.

BEN. Del, Jesus, how can you let him —

(He stops.)

DEL. *(pause)* What? What, Bennett?

BEN. *(beat, then directly to Del)* You know the talk ...

DEL. That I'm in his pocket? I owe him because he was my first major client? Sure, I know. And I knew, all things considered, he'd try to cash his chips one day. So what? Do I tell him to take a hike, I don't want your business? Would you? Would anyone? Hell, no. You get in bed with the guy and you lie real still; and you hope he'll turn away and go to sleep.

BEN. Stand up to him.

DEL. He's my *client*.

BEN. *(strategizing)* I mean the whole firm. At the Monday Partnership Meeting move for a vote of confidence on Grayhawk, I'll second you; a spontaneous uprising, the Will of Partnership.

DEL. (after pondering) You're nuts.

BEN. Exactly; the one thing Sutter'll never expect.

DEL. You think the guy's would back me?

BEN. We have to stop pussy footing around and define ourselves. Are we a firm that allows one client to deny another client equal access to the law because he's rich? Is that what we stand for? Grayhawk can be a referendum on pro bono. We'll put every partner on record with a show of hands. Now's the time!

DEL. And if Sutter dumps us?

BEN. Fuck him. *(a grin)* There's other clients out there.

DEL. *(suddenly maudlin)* That's what Max would say, right? You sound like him. That ... cockiness. I never had it. Walk in a courtroom I'd go blank, no words. I took a course in public speaking ... even tried therapy. I'd have given anything to be a great litigator. Real people, real problems. Instead all I do is stare at a blue screen and daydream. *(vague)* Have you ever been to Tibet?

BEN. — About a vote ...

DEL. *(breaking down)* Sutter killed my marriage, you know. Bled me dry. I never had time with Dierdre and the kids.

BEN. — Del ...

DEL. Personal shit, huh? Chinese Wall. *(shifting gears)* I'll give your suggestion careful consideration, Bennett. Right now I'm in a listening mode, hearing the options, keeping an open mind. Thanks for your recommendation.

(BENNETT is thrown by DEL's sudden formal manner.)

ABE. *(enters briskly)* Is the room free? Oh, Del, thanks for your comments on the Hospice Brief. Would you look over my revisions, they're on your desk ...

DEL. My pleasure.

(DEL starts out.)

BEN. *(following DEL)* Del, wait up —

ABE. These need your signature, Bennett. Do you mind? *(ABE spreads documents. DEL goes. BENNETT remains; offhand)* So you fired a shot across Sutter's bow last night. Sorry to miss *that* party! Of course I don't condone such behavior.

(ABE chuckles.)

BEN. *(at the table)* Where do I sign?

MARGOT. *(Entering, to ABE)* You wanted to see me ... ? *(ABE removes and opens a cigarette case for MARGOT.)* Wasn't this floor declared smoke-free? *(ABE doesn't move. MARGOT takes a cigarette, wondering what he's up to.)* When d'you switch to filters?

ABE. Wife's orders. Fifty years wishing me dead, suddenly she wants me to live forever. Women! *(to MARGOT)* Not you, of course.

BEN. *(by the table)* I don't see anything here for signature.

(ABE paces, thinking how to handle this.)

ABE. Del's recent behavior ... how would you describe it?

BEN. *(a quick glance at MARGOT)* He has a lot on his plate.

ABE. I'm not speaking idly. Is Sutter out to get Grayhawk?

MARGOT. *(brief look at BENNETT)* Bottom line; probably.

ABE. If we stand firm, how does he respond, best guess?

BEN. The Arapaho used to yank out a man's fingernails one by one — Sutter might try something like that, pull his business one case at a time till we cry uncle —

MARGOT. Or he might drop us completely ...

ABE. That's eight million a year; ten-point-seven-four per cent of our revenue. Could we survive?

BEN. It depends.

ABE. On what?

MARGOT. Leadership. *(beat)* Since you ask.

ABE. You think the firm would survive a pay cut that big?

BEN. Anyone here could earn more somewhere else. Money doesn't keep them at D&R, it's something deeper; pride, loyalty. We're a kickass firm. Our best position is back to the wall. *(beat)* Remind the guys what we stand for and they'll take on anyone, even Sutter.

ABE. *(pleased)* Thank you, Bennett. *(He checks the "opening" in the wall, and seeing no one outside, he continues.)* The Stanko trial starts next week in Chicago. I want Del to lead the team.

BEN. Stanko's not his case.

ABE. Del's life right now — Sutter being his client — plus the divorce, terrible business. A change of scene might do him good.

BEN. What's the part you're leaving out?

ABE. The bylaws state — somewhat vaguely, but they can be read to mean — that after a certain number of days physical absence from his office, an officer of the firm can be replaced by a vote of the Board.

BEN. *(pause — stunned)* Dump Del?

ABE. Early retirement.

BEN. Sutter hasn't fired a shot and you're ready to scuttle our chief operations officer less than five months before his term expires, what kind of message does *that* send?

ABE. It leaves Sutter without a friend in Rome. And who we put in Del's place will drive the point home. Look, I know he's your friend ...

BEN. Friendship is not the issue.

ABE. Exactly. What's best for the firm, nothing else matters.

BEN. What's best for the firm is not to panic.

ABE. Del's distracted. He drifts off in mid-thought. It's giving everyone the heebie-jeebies.

BEN. He has a plan, Abe. A very fine one.

ABE. Del has no plan. The firm has no leader. It's time for you to step up, Bennett.

BEN. *(stunned)* Me?

ABE. Of course you, who else are we talking about? The job's yours, do you accept, yes or no?

BEN. *(stunned, then rallying)* Come elections I'll accept every support you offer. But to stab Del in the back? And to take office without a mandate from the Partnership? In you own words, "Invalid power leads to invalid acts," Dine vs. —

ABE. Dine vs. Magruder, I know the case, thank you. And I note your scruples. But they're entirely beside the point ...

BEN. *(suddenly agitated)* Sutter's the only point right now. Not Del, not sending messages. Stop Sutter and the problem goes away.

ABE. And how do we achieve that little miracle?

BEN. *(controlling his agitation)* You'll see Monday night. I think you'll have reason to be very proud of this firm. Now if you'll excuse me, I have business in Wyoming.

ABE. Wyoming?!

BEN. A deposition on Grayhawk.

ABE. At a time like this?!

BEN. Looks promising. Documents. A witness. *(beat)* Sutter's trying to make us panic. Don't let him. Business as usual. That's our posture.

ABE. What's your plan for Monday?

BEN. It's *Del's* plan; ask him, he's Managing Partner. *(glancing at his watch)* And I'm late for my plane.

(He exits.)

ABE. He turned me down! Why?! He's wanted the job since way

before Max quit. He's shown every sign of being ready.

MARGOT. Except a willingness to stab a partner in the back. You were testing his integrity, right?

ABE. You know me better than that. So does he. We need him here rallying partnership against Sutter if that's the plan ... if there *is* a plan, which I very much doubt, the way he ran off ...

MARGOT. *(amused)* Do yourself a favor. Go home, run a bath, listen to opera, cook your wife a nice meal —

ABE. This is no time for him to chase rainbows.

MARGOT. Bennett's the sharpest strategist in the firm. He's ten steps ahead of anything you're worried about. I know it's a hard thing, Abe, but you have to let go. You trained him well. Let him run with it.

ABE. My dear, for fifteen years your assessment of Mr. Traube has been deeply compromised by a mad crush.

(MARGOT fumbles out her cigarettes.)

MARGOT. Go to hell...

(She pats her body in search of a light.)

ABE. Only two reasons a man turns down a chance like this. Either he's afraid, or there's something he wants more. And if that something is in Wyoming, and it's what I think it is, we're in much deeper trouble than I thought.

(ABE lights MARGOT's cigarette, snatches the "NO SMOKING" sign off the table and starts out as the lights fade.)

Scene 2 / Motel Room — Wyoming

(A roadside motel room off the beaten path, curtains across the rear window. Car headlights sweep the curtains. CHRIS parts them and checks outside, then returns to the bed to study documents spread out there. A knock. She moves swiftly to the door and stands tensely for a moment. A second knock.)

CHRIS. *(through door)* Mr. Wofford? *(pause)* Carter?
BEN. *(outside)* It's Bennett.

(Puzzled, CHRIS throws the lock and lets him in.)

CHRIS. Where's VanZant?
BEN. He's behind on some contract work. I'm the only one up to speed on Grayhawk.
CHRIS. Were any cars parked outside? Besides mine?
BEN. *(indicates "no," looking around)* "The Motor Lodge." My, god, I haven't seen homasote walls since dad left the military. Mildewed wallpaper, lino floor. Does LivEarth get a corporate rate here?
CHRIS. My witness choose it.

(BENNETT nervously opens his briefcase.)

BEN. The famous "Mr. Wofford" — who gave you these documents.
CHRIS. Well, left them at reception.
BEN. You've never actually seen him?
CHRIS. He's scared to death. He thinks Reinhardt's having him followed.
BEN. So what do you know about Mr. Curtis Wofford? Family man, employed, criminal record; would he make a credible witness?
CHRIS. He sounded quite articulate on the phone.
BEN. — How long did he talk?
CHRIS. A few minutes. Enough to give me directions to the mo-

tel here —

BEN. Anything else?

CHRIS. *(defensive)* I found a former employer who said he was a hard and dependable worker.

BEN. Who was? Curtis Wofford, or someone using the name Curtis Wofford.

CHRIS. Aren't we being a little melodramatic, Mr. Traube? I'm here for a routine deposition. If it leads somewhere, well —

BEN. This so-called witness has Reinhardt involved in payoffs in Washington, bribery of state officials, extortion, misappropriation of funds, if even half of it's true Rheinhardt's looking at twenty years behind bars —

CHRIS. Dates. Names. Transcripts of phone calls, e-mail, interoffice memos. It doesn't get much better than that.

BEN. Exactly. Never trust pennies from heaven.

CHRIS. You know your problem? You expect things to turn out bad.

BEN. In the legal world it's called preparation.

CHRIS. *(more relaxed)* Well, maybe we caught a break. It happens.

BEN. When's the deposition?

CHRIS. Sometime this week-end. He wouldn't pin it down. He's probably somewhere out there watching.

BEN. Or you're getting the runaround; bogus witness, false documents, anything to waste your time while they score a logging permit. They may even deliver a decoy witness, and how will you figure out if he's for real? What questions will you ask, how do you catch him at a lie, what'd your strategy? This is the major leagues, these guys play for keeps.

CHRIS. Is that why you flew to Wyoming? Damsel in distress, Traube to the rescue!?

BEN. This cute-playful-sarcastic thing of yours is getting real old, Chris. You have a shitload of work to do and no time for games.

CHRIS. Okay, explain why a Senior Partner of D&R came all the way to the middle of nowhere to assist at a deposition?

BEN. I told you —

CHRIS. "Carter's tied up." Not good enough. You could leave

BUYING TIME

me out here twisting in the wind. This isn't your case.

BEN. That depends on our witness —

CHRIS. *(alert)* "Our" witness? Are you taking this case?

BEN. *(nods perfunctorily)* I'm here, aren't I?

CHRIS. Is that official? *(pause, then with genuine gratitude)* Thank you, Mr. Traube. I assume it's your doing?

BEN. You're welcome. And it is. Now let's see if you have enough to get Reinhardt off our back.

CHRIS. "Off our back?" What does *that* mean?

BEN. It means, if your evidence is good, we'll offer to eat it if he leaves the Tuintu forest alone.

CHRIS. Blackmail?

BEN. The legal term is "settlement."

CHRIS. I'm not settling with Reinhardt. I want him, Bennett, I want his operation exposed, I want him behind bars ...

BEN. And I want to get my firm off the hook, okay? His friend Sutter's leaning all over us to drop this case. With something decent to throw back at them we can get both these goons to back off.

CHRIS. And let Reinhardt walk away?

BEN. We save a forest. Not to mention a law firm.

CHRIS. So that's the rules now. They bribe, and bully, and make deals under the table and if we catch them, what's the worst that can happen? Punishment? No, no, nothing that clear. The terrible price they pay is being forced to *make a deal*. And lay low for a few months before they're up to their old tricks again. That's why I've devoted my life to the law; so I can join the club one day and play the game by their rules —

BEN. *(irritated)* You've made your point.

CHRIS. No, Bennett. If I had, you wouldn't be talking deals. I know how much you hate these people. You built a career fighting them. And I know it makes you sick that they always end up calling the shots, isn't that why you lost it at Sutter's house?

BEN. Who told you?

CHRIS. It's the talk of Mesa. He fed you off paper plates; he thinks your firm's a joke. Maybe he's right.

(CHRIS moves suddenly to the window, parts the curtains a crack and

looks out.)

BEN. *(beat)* You want to save a forest, I want Sutter off my back. It's a good result. Your way means years in court, decades maybe, fighting not just Reinhardt, trust me, he's only the part that shows; an action this big'll take you way underground where all these guys are tangled at the roots; mining, timber, ranchers; the entire extractive mafia — with money enough to tie you up in motions 'til the end of time, and what does *your* war chest look like? There's not a law firm on earth who'd go the distance with this.

CHRIS. There's one.

BEN. After three years against the Governor, forget it. We can't take on another Goliath the morning after.

CHRIS. One good deed buys a year of making money? More — five years, ten, what's the exchange rate on a virtuous act these days ... ?

BEN. God save us from the righteous with nothing to lose.

CHRIS. *(an outburst)* Don't patronize me, Bennett. *(controlling tears)* You have no idea what I have to lose here.

BEN. You want revenge on Reinhardt for clear-cutting your Happy Place, sorry, that doesn't rock my world.

CHRIS. — what I have to lose? I'll tell you. The kind of lawyer I always wanted to be is you; good enough to work anywhere and get rich but instead went his own way. You know what it means to see one person hold out when the rest line up at the feedbag? I thought you could show me how it's done, how to balance a decent life with honorable law. I understand cutting deals, Bennett, it's something you do when you're years into litigation and worn out from the fight, but to lay down your weapons before the battle even starts ...

(BENNETT, after watching her for a moment, rises.)

BEN. All right, Chris, listen to me. If the documents you sent to my office are your entire case ... a few dozen pages of Xeroxes, and two minutes on the phone with god knows who; it could be anyone — Reinhardt setting you up, a crank who hates loggers ... it's total garbage.

CHRIS. *(pause)* Then why are you here?
BEN. Because — *(beat)* I don't know.
CHRIS. *(unmoored)* Oh.

(Agitated, BENNETT starts to pace, rubbing his scalp, as if trying to shape the chaos inside.)

BEN. *(beat)* I was offered something today — something huge.
CHRIS. If you came to celebrate, sorry, I'm not in the mood.
BEN. *(beat)* Chris, there was a note with these documents Carter gave me saying where you'd be this weekend. Did you ask him to put it in the envelope?
CHRIS. Why?
BEN. Did you want me to know where to find you? Did you hope I'd come?
CHRIS. To have expert help deposing a potential witness, of course —
BEN. I was offered Managing Partner this morning, and I turned it down because *(searching)* — because —
CHRIS. *(impressed)* You turned down Managing Partner?
BEN. Oh, the offer stands, I can say yes tomorrow if I want ... but if I did *take charge* ... if I really went for it ...
CHRIS. *(excited)* You'd be brilliant!
BEN. Chris, any fool can hold office, but to *lead* ... how do you know you can do it, inspire a group of incredibly bright people with responsibilities to sacrifice income and hang together through god knows what? That takes trust, faith, passion — I'm talking mysteries here, things that don't have words, it's what you said, most of what we do is irrational in the end and I don't know how to reckon things in that realm. How do I know I have it in me to lead D&R through what could turn into a decade-long action against — *(suddenly)* oh, man, wouldn't it be a be a trip to nail Rheinhardt! Max could do it. Del, never.
CHRIS. And you?
BEN. Ten years ago I wouldn't have thought twice. *(beat)* Now — I don't know.
CHRIS. I want to act but I have no skills. You have all the weap-

ons, but you won't fight. No wonder the Reinhardts always win.

BEN. I need a sign that I should jump, Chris. An omen, anything, a burning bush ... a note in an envelope. This may sound strange to you — it does to me, I mean, I'm a very analytical person by nature — but on the flight up I found myself reading my horoscope in the Air West magazine. I never do that. "A time to trust your instincts," it said. And there's me thinking — me, this utterly rational person — "maybe her note is the sign I've been looking for, maybe she wants me there, maybe she senses some thing in me, that *thing*, the "it," the magic, maybe I have it after all, if I just make one bold move for a change, one fucking leap into the unknown instead of fretting the details, weighing options — *(laughs)* Or maybe I'm going nuts!

CHRIS. *(careful)* Are you asking me if you should take the job?

BEN. Among other things.

CHRIS. Of course. You're the obvious choice. They'd lucky to have you.

BEN. You'd be lucky, too; if I led the firm. And you were my client.

CHRIS. *(admitting)* It did cross my mind.

BEN. *(sudden focus)* You're flirting with me, aren't you.

CHRIS. I beg your pardon?

BEN. Right from the start, "if you weren't married yes I'd have a drink."

CHRIS. If that's what you think this is all about, you'd better leave right now.

BEN. Stop being coy, Chris. We're in way too deep to play games. Should I take over the firm? Was your note an invitation?

CHRIS. Those are two separate issues.

BEN. They're exactly the same. You understand danger, right; your wild place; well, here we are, and we're both scared to death because what happens now could change everything. I'm ready to jump. What about you?

CHRIS. *(standing, awkward and vulnerable.)* I never meant for this to turn — personal.

BEN. *(a new energy)* Is that why I was the topic of discussion with your roomie? "He doesn't look that old."

CHRIS. I'm no good at intimacy. It never happens when it's supposed to, and it always gets messy. *(vulnerable)* Bennett, are you very sure this is what you want?

BEN. *(amazed)* It *was* an invitation. I was *right*!

CHRIS. *(quiet, vulnerable, afraid now)* Yes, I wanted you to come, damn it. *I* put the note there hoping — *(pause)* I'm glad you're here.

BEN. *(moving closer to her)* That's all I needed to hear.

CHRIS. Now what?

BEN. *(stops)* We wait for Wofford.

CHRIS. And when he shows up ... ?

BEN. *(moves forward)* First things first.

CHRIS. Can we win without these documents?

BEN. You never stop, do you?

CHRIS. Can we?

BEN. *(moving towards her)* First things first.

(They stand close and kiss gently, exploring something new between them. A noise.)

CHRIS. *(listening, then)* False alarm. *(she turns to him)* Just so you know; if this goes any farther, I could become a real big problem in your life.

BEN. You already are.

*(She unslips his tie and they fall back in bed.
The lights fade.)*

Scene 3 / Partner's Lounge —Donne & Russo

(MARGOT waits at a card table. HAL enters.)

HAL. *(irate)* Un-fucking-believable! They're hauling our files out of the building and where's Security; watching tapes of the Young & The Fucking Restless while Sutter's hired goons steal our property.

MARGOT. "Impound" is the word. On Sutter's orders. He's taking us off the Jessup Mine Collapse.

HAL. Our biggest cash cow. Terrific. This is, as my kid says, totally not my day.

MARGOT. *(to herself)* Like the Arapaho; one fingernail at a time.

HAL. There's got to be something we can offer him before we lose all his business —

MARGOT. I think he's made himself clear, hon; it's drop Grayhawk or drop dead.

HAL. So it's plan B. Did you talk to Pete, is he with us?

(As PETE enters through the gap.)

MARGOT. We'll know soon enough —

PETE. Any bright ideas how to stop the circus out there, that's a million a year going down the elevator, why isn't Del in touch with Sutter?

MARGOT. Sutter's out of town.

PETE. Bull. He's been driving around all day in that yellow convertible of his —

HAL. Waving his Stetson at passers-bye, howdee folks; yes, we know. But for us, he's out of town, ho-ho.

PETE. This is bughouse. Why's he making so much noise? He can't expect us to drop the case with everyone watching.

MARGOT. Unless everyone watching is just what he wants.

PETE. What does he gain by that?

MARGOT. With our record on the environment, get real? We're

a test case.

HAL. For what?

MARGOT. Lumber, mining, ranchers ... *(hesitant - is this a good time?)* I've found a pattern; four years ago, out of the blue, they started hiring environmental firms like us, firms who won big actions against them. Remember Sutter approaching Del, of all people, a guy fresh from litigation, no major clients before —

HAL. — Or since ...

PETE. Del got lucky. It happens.

MARGOT. No, Pete; I cross-referenced thirty-eight law firms statewide; names dates, client sheets. The pattern is unmistakable.

PETE. That's preposterous.

MARGOT. Once we depend on the income, we're in their pocket. We do what they say, or they threaten to pull out. The tail wags the dog.

PETE. Paranoid fantasy. Pure speculation.

MARGOT. I fought it for months, but no other scenario works. Plus it's smart; hard to prove, no fingerprints ...

HAL. It's the most deviously underhand, ratfuck scheme I ever —

PETE. Hal, could you make a big effort to complete one thought without obscenities.

HAL. *(beat)* If those scurvy knaves have our collective gonads in their grubby little paws I'll be darned steamed.

PETE. Here's why you have to be wrong. 'Cause if not, there ain't a thing we can do to stop them using that leverage. Not now, not ever.

MARGOT. We can fight back. We can rally corporate and promise Del complete support on a vote for Grayhawk.

PETE. Why would he allow a vote against his own client?

MARGOT. Because it's that or surrender Grayhawk. And a big NO hands the problem back to Sutter.

PETE. What problem, he'll just drop us.

MARGOT. And lose everything? *(All are puzzled)* These guys are trying to *control* us from *inside.* If we vote for Grayhawk Sutter loses that control. He fails. Their plan falls apart and every firm has our example to follow. It's a risk, I admit. But it's bold, unexpected, very D&R.

PETE. Right; the perfect Jim Jones move, collective suicide. "If you love Grayhawk shout Amen and pass the Cool Aid."

HAL. *(pause)* Come on, Pete, solidarity. Del's going to need us. Can you deliver corporate?

PETE. *(morose)* You don't need our vote. We're the minority section. You need our revenue, of course —

HAL. *(exploding)* Oh, fuck off —

MARGOT. Girls, girls!

HAL. — I've taken enough shit about corporate bankrolling the firm; your guys earn big off *our* reputation, it's litigators who put D&R on the map —

MARGOT. — Hormone check —

HAL. — Without us —

MARGOT. — step off it, Hal —

HAL. No, god damn it, the corporate section's a bunch of whiners who were mostly turned down by every high-end firm in America...

PETE. And you wonder why my guys resent you arrogant bastards sneering down at us from your moral high horse, a horse paid for with our big bad corporate dollars ...

MARGOT. Oh, look, a crisis; watch us pull together!

DEL. *(Enter briskly)* Thank you for coming in. I'm sorry to mess up your week-end, but we have —

PETE. What's going on with the Jessup files — ?

DEL. Never mind Jessup. Ten partners in corporate just threatened to quit if Sutter walks.

PETE. Corporate's my section, why didn't they come to me?

DEL. Never mind protocol —

PETE. I *do* mind. Am I head of corporate or not?

HAL. Margot found something you should know about. Tell him, Margot ...

DEL. Not now, Hal ...

HAL. This is way bigger than we thought —

DEL. *(frazzled)* Just please — be quiet and let me speak. Every firm in town is chasing Sutter's business.

PETE. Who threatened to quit, I want names ...

DEL. *(explodes)* SHUT UP, for Christ sakes. All of you, just for-

BUYING TIME 63

get your god damn petty turf wars for a moment and work with me here. *(beat)* I'm sorry. Pete, I'm — I'm ...

MARGOT. *(reassuringly)* You're in a terrible situation, we all sympathize. Whatever you have to do, we're behind you. *(to others)* Right Hal? Pete?

DEL. Thank you, Margot.

MARGOT. Absolutely.

DEL. *(with difficulty)* Because what I propose is going to be misunderstood in some quarters.

MARGOT. We're with you. Here's some research that might bring people to our side.

DEL. This firm is my life. If we have to close our doors, we lose everything, including Rule 7. I called you here to ask — and it's the most painful decision I've ever had to make — please, at the Partnership Meeting Monday night, support my motion to drop the Grayhawk case.

HAL. *(after a long pause)* Del ... no!

MARGOT. *(lighting a cigarette)* I'm sorry, I have to smoke.

HAL. I'm in shock, man. I'm in total fucking shock. This would never happen if Max were here.

MARGOT. Or Bennett.

DEL. Bennett's in Wyoming. *I'm* here.

MARGOT. Everyone's expecting a vote to *keep* Grayhawk.

DEL. I'm offering the same choice.

MARGOT. With big red arrows pointing to the dumpster. Not very subtle, Delmore.

PETE. What's our argument? Without a conflict of interest, how do we scuttle a client without cause?

DEL. The legal theory is called "positional conflict of interest."

MARGOT. Where did you dig *that* one up?

HAL. If you want to make us look like clowns, pass out red noses and we'll walk around town going *(yokel voice)* "Oh, now I remember, positional conflict of interest, doy-dee, doy-dee, doy."

DEL. *(continuing doggedly)* Positional conflict often arises well into initial research on a case due to —

MARGOT. Bippity-boppety-boo!

DEL. NEVER MIND, OKAY!!! Never mind the *reason*. Dropping the case will be viewed as a prudent and necessary action; the firm'll be safe. And most important, Rule 7, as a principle, will survive.

HAL. We'll be whores Monday night and wake Tuesday virgins ...

MARGOT. *(lighter)* Like Doris Day.

HAL. Doris Day! Whatever happened to Doris Day?!

DEL. Go ahead, joke, laugh; it won't bring back the days of pot and whiskey and all nighters at The Wells. It was a beautiful time. I miss it, too. But now we have eighty-seven partners to consider; ninety-four associates, one hundred and eighty plus support staff with mortgages, tuition, health insurance ... alimony. I will not risk eight million plus dollars on a god damn *bird*!

PETE. *(starts out)* My daughter has ballet at 4:00. Excuse me.

DEL. Pete, will you back me?

PETE. I don't care about pro bono. Sorry, I just don't. It's church work. You gotta choose, warriors; a BMW or the holy stigmata, not both. I know you think old cynical Pete, he's with D&R because deep down *he cares*; he'd rather represent Mother Theresa than Saddam Hussein. Wrong. I'm a Doctor of Law. I operate on clients. How well I did the job and how much I earned, that's all that matters. See, I like making money. I really do. That's what I like.

DEL. *(unsure)* So I have your vote, right?

PETE. No. Sorry.

DEL. Why not?

PETE. We took the case, we can't drop it. I'm not being high minded, just legally exact. Have a nice week end.

(PETE exits.)

HAL. *(sings)* TWO BOTTLES OF BEER ON THE WALL / TWO BOTTLES OF BEER... *(speaks)* That should be the easy one. If *he* didn't bite — Del, let's at least come out of this with some dignity.

DEL. If we come out at all we can worry about dignity.

HAL. The hookers downtown have a motto, "If you got the money, honey, I got the time." Kinda like lawyers, come to think of it. Except there's tricks even they won't do for money. Let's try rising to

their level, shall we?
DEL. I intend to win this vote, with or without your support.

(HAL leaves the room. A pause.)

MARGOT. *(turning to DEL)* You promised Sutter the case.
DEL. Careful, Margot.
MARGOT. Have you forgotten who your friends are?
DEL. Friends don't hold secret meetings about your removal from office.
MARGOT. So the walls have ears. Did they mention that Bennett took your side. He's trying to help you.
DEL. Really? I think he's trying to feel superior. Extending sympathy to a second rate lawyer? Who's personal life is a disaster, whatever — no, don't bother defending him, Margot. His opinion of me is immaterial. I have no illusions about myself, about anything, really. Not any more. Which is why I can do what has to be done. It's my little comfort, you might say ... knowing I'm the one person in the firm who can get us through this mess whole.
MARGOT. Drop Grayhawk and every lawyer worth a damn will leave.
DEL. Brave talk. We'll see. This is a no smoking area. Put that out.

DEL waits. MARGOT douses her cigarette in a coffee mug. DEL goes.)

Scene 4 / The Traube Dinning/Living Room

(JOBETH sits at an antique table with a notebook, tulip glass and a half empty bottle of vintage wine. A car door slams outside.
Pause.
BENNETT enters with his overnight bag and watches JO. She knows he's there, but doesn't look up.)

BEN. *(pause)* We landed late, I had to swing by the office. *(glances at his watch)* Sorry.

JOBETH. *(not looking up)* Our marriage is worth just over one point nine million dollars, did you know that? *(explains)* "Statement of Joint Assets." For the re-mortgage.

(Sips wine.)

BEN. *(reading wine bottle)* The good stuff. Are we celebrating?

JOBETH. *(avoiding)* There's a ton of messages. Del. Margot. Hal. Some major crisis at work — you didn't tell me. I remember a time — !

BEN. Jo, what's wrong ...?

JOBETH. *(too quickly)* How was Montana?

BEN. Wyoming.

JOBETH. Whatever.

BEN. We have to talk.

JOBETH. I'm listening.

BEN. *(pause)* Not like this. Take tomorrow off. We used to do that, remember; talk all day?

JOBETH. I remember.

BEN. *(beat)* I've done something very stupid.

JOBETH. *(pause) Have* you?

BEN. Wyoming was a bust. A witness didn't show. Jo, there's something I have to do.

JOBETH. *(bracing for the worst)* Talk about *us*, Bennett.

BEN. There is no "us" any more; no *me*, anyway. Do you have any idea how long it's been since anything I did felt *real*!?

JOBETH. What are you *saying*, Bennett? What do you *want*?!

BEN. I'm taking over the firm. Now. No campaign, no kissing Corporate's ass. I'm going to replace Del and take D&R back to what made us great — every client welcome, money or no. I want you with me, Beth. But partners are going to quit. We'll have hard years ahead.

JOBETH. Is this take it or leave it?

BEN. Yes; keeping us together can't be my excuse any more.

JOBETH. *(long pause)* Well, well. My brave warrior! *(almost cracking)* A toast, darling. To "Newfound Courage" — and whoever inspired it.

BEN. *(worried, clinking glasses)* Are you drunk?

JOBETH. *(suddenly playful)* Tell me the truth. Wasn't it really Sylvia Lukas you wanted to dance with that night?

BEN. Sylvia — ?

JOBETH. I saw you watching us across the Pizzaporium, me and Sylvia, remember? Scared to make your move, but Jay Hinkle was at your table so you had to try. When Sylvia didn't see you coming towards her you pretended you'd come over to dance with *me*, isn't that right?

BEN. Jay Hinkle, the quarterback? I was hanging with Jay that fall, god!

JOBETH. The girls all wanted Jay. And the boys wanted Sylvia Lukas. But you got me. And I got you, babe.

BEN. *(afraid now, hiding behind levity)* Wine always makes you maudlin.

JOBETH. *(controlled rage)* How could you violate our pact?

BEN. Pact?

JOBETH. I praise your work. You praise my charm. But it's understood you'll always be second to someone else, Jay Hinkle, Max, whoever; and I'll always be a notch below the most desirable woman in the room. Wasn't that understood — our terrible secret? How could you violate the rules like that? To chase dreams of, what? Being number one? Dancing with you that night I thought; "Bennett Traube, why haven't I noticed him before, this fine and decent man who can't play football so he borrows glory hanging with the heroes. We're so alike; we're everyone's second choice, and we could be so happy if we never violate that truth." *(sudden rage)* BENNETT!!! *(hands him a manila envelope)* This was on the driveway yesterday. Excuse me.

(She exits, slightly unsteady with wine. He removes eight-by-ten black and white glossies from the envelope and freezes. JOBETH returns with a suitcase. Some clean shirts. Underwear. Socks.)

BEN. Noises outside! Jesus.
JOBETH. She's so *young*, Bennett. Blonde, though; they age faster.
BEN. Is this all? No note?
JOBETH. *(then under control)* Please go. I'm barely holding on.
BEN. Reinhardt set the whole thing up!
JOBETH. If it's blackmail, I'll deny the pictures exist, I'll say I had them made as a joke. What an ugly world you work in.
BEN. I'll get a room in town. *(pause)* May I see the kids?
JOBETH. *(harrowing)* LEAVE US ALONE! *(She breaks down sobbing. BENNETT moves to comfort her. She holds out a hand, like a traffic cop stopping cars; quietly)* No more, Bennett. It's over.

(Lights fade.)

Scene 5 / The Wells/Partner's Meeting Hall

(A split set: Behind, a long table on a raised platform representing the head table of the Partner's meeting at D&R, and also the "bar" of The Wells, who's logo is a bucket-and-winch over a well.)
Downstage, a jukebox, a dance floor and some tables. Lights shift back and forth to define the "active area," and actors left in the "dark" freeze in place until their action resumes.
At start: jukebox plays quiet rock-a-billy. CARTER and CHRIS dance. CHRIS barely moves.)

BUYING TIME

CARTER. You want to just stand there and daydream while I dance by myself?

CHRIS. Sorry, it's ... Bennett.

CARTER. They're meeting, and there's not a blessed thing more we can do right now except keep our fingers crossed.

CHRIS. I don't know what happened; Wyoming was so amazing; he told me everything about himself, his dreams, his plans; we were totally connected.

CARTER. I bet you were ...

CHRIS. Now I don't know what he wants. Maybe he's numb from leaving home or something ... When I try to get through it's like Wyoming never happened and god I hate this emotional stuff ...

(A cricket noise. CARTER pulls out a cell phone.)

CARTER. Here we go, live from D&R ... *(phone:)* Lane, *que pasa, amigo?* No, we're already at The Wells. Yeah, she's here with me. What's going on, have they started yet ... ?

(During this, the sound of applause fades up and lights rise on the chairs in back, where DEL enters with PETE, HAL and BENNETT. Lights fade in The Wells.)

DEL. I call to order this meeting of Partnership, Monday, July Ten. Let the minutes note I have entered a motion for us to cease representing LivEarth in the matter of Grayhawk vs. Reinhardt Paper Industries. Mr. Traube has asked to address the meeting. Bennett ...

BEN. Thank you, Del, everyone — for the chance to speak. *(takes out his speech)* "Partners of Donne & Russo ..."

(He stares at the room for a moment.)

DEL. *(waiting, and then)* Bennett ...

BEN. *(shakes his head)* It's no use. I spent all weekend on a speech defending Grayhawk. But standing before you now, esteemed colleagues, life-long friends who face a very hard choice, I realize I have no case. *(He puts the speech down on his chair and turns back to the meeting.)* Del is right. Keeping Grayhawk makes no sense. We stand to lose major money. Big clients. The income graph someone hung on the back wall even shows us having to close our doors. The risk is unacceptable. So let's find our client a good, high-end firm like D&R, and wish them luck. Of course that firm may have their own Sutter, who dislikes environmental clients. So LivEarth will have to go shopping again. And again. And ultimately they will lose to Reinhardt for lack of skilled counsel. But is that really our problem? Del says no. So the Tuintu Forest will become match sticks and greeting cards. Why should we try and stop that from happening? Just because we swore to represent LivEarth to the fullest extent of the law? Because we gave our word, each and every one of us when we interviewed here, to protect Rule 7? Is our word, our oath any reason to risk living at a mere six times the national average instead of ten, because that's the real dimension of the threat, not those four-color charts Del hung in back to scare you. Yes, we're at risk. And that risk, Del says, is unacceptable. It's no reason to defend Grayhawk. *(pause)* Unless. Unless. Unless any small corner of us is not for sale. Like what we stand for, like our pledge to Rule 7, our self respect, our promise to a client. You see, that's really what's at stake tonight, our faith in who we are. *Time Magazine* called us the brightest point of light on the moral compass of the law today. I always thought D&R was unique. I don't know about you, but that's why *I've* worked here, and not somewhere else, for twenty years. I love the law. I love it with all my heart. *(he controls his tears)* That's why I chose to practice where what we believe in means more than what we earn. If money brings you to the law, there's no end of firms ready to welcome you with open arms. Apply, name your price, be happy. But get the hell out of *my* firm. Because here, we honor our legal obligation to every client who walks through the door, even when it's dangerous. Because, god damn it, *here* that is who *we* are. That is what *we* do. If you don't like it, if you feel as Del does, you don't belong here. Get out. But if you believe in what we represent, vote for Grayhawk. If we win tonight, I promise you, the greatest days of Donne & Russo lie ahead.

(Light applause. Then it swells ... and swells.)

BUYING TIME 71

DEL. *(stands)* May we have quiet. Quiet, please. Do you yield the floor? *(BENNETT nods)* The income projections in back were prepared by an outside accounting firm, let the record show. Now I'll ask Bennett to leave the meeting.

BEN. Why?

DEL. You attached yourself to the LivEarth defense. This vote concerns your case, and you're forbidden to vote on issues effecting a client you represent — *(booing from the floor)* — it's in the bylaws, Number 26, subsection "C" *(waves pamphlet)* You'll find copies in the rear ...

BEN. Sutter is forcing this vote and he's *your* client. If I go, you go with me ...

DEL. This case is Reinhardt vs. LivEarth. Sutter has no connection.

BEN. *(over loud booing)* I move we both have to leave ...

DEL. You may not enter further business while there's a motion on the floor —

BEN. Don't insult our intelligence, Del. We're both up to our neck here. I'm willing, if you are, for a neutral third party to decide who goes.

DEL. Which neutral third party did you have in mind?

BEN. We're voting the future of the firm. I'd call the man who mentored our generation of leadership, Abe Einhorn. Do you agree?

DEL. *(a beat)* Absolutely.

(Applause. BENNETT expected DEL to object. DEL rises to join the applause for ABE, who's making his progress to the podium. ALL pay tribute to their elder statesman as ABE takes the floor.)

ABE. I thank Bennett for a rousing and heartfelt speech. His words, his sentiments, his *passions* will linger here I feel confident, with or without his reassuring presence. In light of the explosive issue before us, I suggest we stand behind our Managing Partner and let him rule on procedure.

(Confusion from the floor. HAL starts to protest.)

DEL. *(quickly)* May I have a second on the motion to —

BEN. *(restraining HAL)* Never mind! *(to the meeting)* I take Abe's point. We've had enough divisiveness. I'll respect the bylaws. We all know what the vote has to be.

(He exits.)

HAL. *(standing)* Let the minutes note that the head of Litigation voted to keep Grayhawk then followed Mr. Traube in protest.

(He exits. Loud shouts of protest. ABE holds up a hand.)

ABE. You all know my sympathies. Here is my sealed vote. *(hands envelope to DEL)* Mr. Gregorian is my proxy. The rest I leave in his capable and energetic hands.

(ABE exits.
The Wells — BENNETT enters. CHRIS and CARTER approach him. The WAITER comes from in back.)

CHRIS. Any news ... ?
BEN. I'm cautiously optimistic.
HAL. *(bursting in)* Double bourbon rocks. Make it triple. That devious fuck. For a fiver I'd have him greased, I'm serious, I've defended clients who owe me one ...
BEN. Hal, take your finger off the trigger; Abe was brilliant. He doesn't need to take a position in public, he *wrote* Rule 7, everyone knows were he stands on Grayhawk.
HAL. Wake the fuck up, man. He cut you off at the knees. *(to CHRIS and CARTER)* This guy gives a killer speech, then Abraham the one-horned-fucking-goat rears up on his hind legs and pulls the rug out.

(ABE has entered with a paper sack. He overhears this, but ignores it.)

ABE. Waiter. My usual.
WAITER. Sir, I don't know your usual.

BEN. Bourbon and tonic with a twist. Make it two.

(ABE, with regal composure, sits at a table and puts down the sack. BENNETT approaches with concern.)

BEN. They voted?
ABE. Not yet.
BEN. You left the meeting?
ABE. Sit down, Bennett. *(he obeys)* Superb speech.

(There's an edginess between them.)

BEN. Who's side are you on, Abe?
ABE. I'm on the side of survival. Without Sutter's business we die. But keeping it means we have to stab ourselves in the heart. How's that for a paradox? To live, we have to commit a kind of suicide.
BEN. Leadership is all we need.
ABE. Del spent the last seventy-two hours rallying the firm. He showed surprising character.
BEN. He's a frightened mediocrity who lost his vision of the law and has nothing left to live for except power, and he'll sacrifice anything keep it.
ABE. Why didn't you talk this way last Friday?
BEN. I'm a wiser man today. I accept your offer.
ABE. It's withdrawn.
BEN. Why?
ABE. Forget Managing Partner. It would break your heart.
BEN. Try me.
ABE. I did. You chose Wyoming.
BEN. I had a way out of this mess; documents, a witness.
ABE. You had nothing. When the firm needed you, you ran. How can you expect them to trust you after that? All your speeches, all the fine words in the world, they're just —

(He leaves it hanging.)

BEN. What?

ABE. *(waving it off)* No point.

BEN. Tell me. My words are all *what*?

ABE. A smokescreen. Behind it, I'm sorry to say this, but I don't think you really know *what* you believe in. You make rousing speeches, but in the end it's not what the firm stands for, it's the feeling of righteousness you love. When you're faced with real power — the messy compromises, the dirty work — you waver, you hesitate, then run.

BEN. One bad call, Abe. That's all we're talking about here. If I'd been right about Wyoming, we'd be celebrating.

ABE. You're talking heroics, Bennett. Not life. Maybe that's it, I always wondered about your gang, the way you burst on the scene, such *energy*, such *spirit*! I had great hopes. Maybe all it was was posturing. Maybe that's why you all petered out and left the field to workhorses like — what did you call Del? — a determined mediocrity!

BEN. You're backing Del because we disappointed you?

ABE. Because he'll see us through.

BEN. Survival at all costs?

ABE. I see better times ahead. Not in my life, perhaps, but one day some new young Turk's enter the firm, find Rule 7 buried in the bylaws, and breath it back to life. Yes, for now, survival at all costs.

BEN. My time is now, Abe. I have good years left to do law, and I want to practice in a firm that's alive and vital. Most of D&R feels the same. They're behind me.

ABE. We'll know when the votes are counted, won't we? *(The WAITER brings ABE his drink;* standing*)* I'll deal with the photographs. Blackmail was crude of them. You're a good man, Bennett. You're just not a leader.

(ABE sips the drink and starts out.)

WAITER. Sir! You can't take that outside, it's against the law.

ABE. For the drive home, son. Less tonic next time.

(ABE leaves, BENNETT following.)

WAITER. *(following ABE to the door)* The glass ... !!!

BEN. *(turns)* In the sack. He always brings it back clean.

(BENNETT goes out after ABE. The WAITER hurries to the sack and finds the clean glass as:
Lights up on the meeting, where pandemonium reigns. DEL is trying to quiet the uproar with a gavel.)

DEL. Please, everyone, we can't continue without — I must have order. *(stands)* ORDER, ORDER, ORDER, GODDAMN IT. *(stunned silence; DEL continues to stand)* We're going in circles. Here's how it comes down. We can vote for Grayhawk and risk closing our doors. Or vote it down and answer to our conscience. It's a decision no one should have to make. However, there *is* a third option available ... which involves the Steering Committee. Ms. Davis, would you be kind enough to read out paragraph 14, subsection "J" on page 28 of the bylaws ...

(Lights down on meting and up on The Wells, where CARTER is talking on the phone. BENNETT re-enters.)

CARTER. Bennett, something's happening over there. *(hands him phone, explaining)* It's Lane on the line.

(PETE hurries in followed by MARGOT, who carries some loose paper.)

PETE. *(upset)* Waiter, milk and Pepsi. If I can just get through tonight without a drink ...!
MARGOT. *(to the room)* It's over. They voted not to vote.
CHRIS. Is that good or bad?
PETE. It's some bylaw.
MARGOT. If a motion gets bogged down in debate the Managing Partner can call for a vote not to vote, which sends the matter to committee for final action.
PETE. And that's what they did. 71 to 16.
BEN. What committee?
PETE. Steering.

BEN. The *Steering* Committee? They're for house-keeping stuff, not major policy. It's a rubber stamp for Del.

PETE. The old man said follow Del.

BEN. *(stunned)* They voted to drop Grayhawk!?

HAL. They voted for *Del* to drop it. He read them like a book. They want Sutter's money, but they couldn't come out and vote their pocketbooks after your speech. He got them off the hook on a technicality.

WAITER. *(returns with PETE's drink)* Who had the Pepsi?

CARTER. On behalf of the junior associates of Donne and Russo, I hereby name this The Week of the Resume. Oh, where to apply; decisions, decisions ...

(DEL enters. All eyes follow him.)

DEL. Bennett, a word?

BEN. I'm going to challenge the Steering Committee before you meet.

DEL. We just convened.

BEN. Jesus, Del. Not like this. Have a little shame.

DEL. Ms. Martel, I regret to inform you that D&R, after careful consideration -

CHRIS. How long is careful, two minutes?

DEL. We'll of course help you find alternate counsel.

BEN. You just destroyed what took twenty years to build.

DEL. Careful, Bennett.

BEN. Fuck *you*, careful; you sold us out when we could have won.

DEL. And fuck you for thinking the firm means any more to you than it does to me. Do you have any idea what *I've* been through, eating Sutter's shit?! *(enraged)* I JUST SAVED THIS GOD DAMNED FIRM; 360 PEOPLE WITH 360 JOBS. And how I see it, all you did is make a beautiful speech and fuck some girlie in Wyoming.

(BENNETT attacks DEL. They fight fiercely, sloppily.)

CARTER. *(pulling them apart)* Come on, cowboys, that's enough ...

HAL. Del, get a grip.
DEL. *(stops fighting; pause)* Take the week off.

(He exits.)

HAL. I'll see if he's okay. Even assholes have feelings.

(HAL exits.)

PETE. You know, it just occurred to me; if Sutter's been trying to humiliate us from the get-go, this vote leaves us wide open for the sucker punch of all time.

(PETE exits.)

CARTER. *(to BENNETT)* If you keep the case as outside business, I'll be happy to assist. *(hugs CHRIS)* Good night. *(indicates BENNETT)* Good luck.

(He leaves. MARGOT sits across the room, adjusting her makeup while she eaves drops on:

BEN. I'm sorry, Christine.
CHRIS. I don't care about the case right now ...
BEN. You have to apply for Clayton's job, make sure LivEarth keeps the heat under Grayhawk -
CHRIS. Could we talk about this later?
BEN. *(pressing on)* Work is how I cope. I'll teach you the basics. Hell, at this rate I might even apply.
CHRIS. *(resigned to his preoccupation)* Wouldn't that be great gossip, you and me in the same firm ...
BEN. Who cares; everyone knows about us by now.
CHRIS. Are you serious? It wouldn't bother you, us together in the same — ? *(beat)* Because Carter mentioned, with all the turmoil at D&R, there might be some openings soon. What if I interviewed? How would you feel?
BEN. After they threw you to the sharks? How would *you* feel?

CHRIS. I screwed up a routine case; I let Carter talk to the press. I walked into an obvious trap. I need experience. A few years at D&R, I'd have all the lawyering skills I need to be effective.

BEN. *(pause)* You already applied, didn't you?

CHRIS. Carter thinks I'd be crazy not to.

BEN. You're good, Chris. You're *really* good. You just take off your blindfold and find the way.

CHRIS. You have no right to judge me for wanting what you already have. *(then)* Come to my place. We can fight and yell and spend our first bad night together.

BEN. I don't think so.

CHRIS. *(angry now)* At least I'm trying to make it work.

BEN. I'll call you tomorrow.

CHRIS. You know what I think. Del didn't win. You lost.

(She exits.)

MARGOT. *(joins BENNETT, handing him a sheet of paper)* You forgot your speech. I peeked. It's word for word what you said at the meeting. I'm impressed.

(She sits and hands him another document.)

BEN. What's this?

MARGOT. It was on the main fax line after the meeting. I didn't have the heart to tell anyone, not tonight.

BEN. *(reading the fax)* Sutter's dropping D&R. Unbelievable!

MARGOT. Poetic justice. We should hang it in the lobby, with a caption; "At D&R We Aim Low and Miss."

BEN. The sucker punch.

MARGOT. Why'd you turn down Abe's offer?

BEN. *(beat)* What's weird is I don't feel anything. I see exactly what happened; I ran. I let everyone down; my firm, my family, myself. I was afraid, Margot. *(he smiles)* Shouldn't it feel bad to know that about yourself? Maybe a little devastating. In that area?

MARGOT. *(worried, trying levity)* Now for the good news: we'll survive. We'll become a normal law firm, suits for hire. It's a good

health plan. *(serious)* You're a great attorney, Bennett ... well liked, well respected ...
BEN. The best possible second choice. *(And now it all comes crashing down on him.)* Oh, Jesus, Margot, how could I let it happen?!

(MARGOT wants to comfort him, but his pain is so intense, she can't move. Finally BENNETT gains control. MARGOT takes a drink and rises nervously.)

MARGOT. Come on, let's drive around. Maybe a destination'll spring to mind. You shouldn't be alone tonight.
BEN. I'm okay. I'm fine. Really. I'm okay. You're okay. Everything's okay. Chinese Wall. I'll see you tomorrow.

(MARGOT makes a small move towards him, then withdraws, and leaves The Wells. The WAITER approaches with a bill.)

WAITER. Looks like they stuck you with the bill.
BEN. I'll pay.
WAITER. I know we're supposed to give you guys credit, but the boss says no more cause we're about to close. *(starting off)* This old place is coming down next week, can you believe it?
BEN. For a shopping mall.
WAITER. So you heard about it.

(The WAITER is gone. BENNETT is alone now.)

BEN. Sure. *(relishing the irony)* We did the contracts!

(He reaches for a drink, seems unable to complete the gesture and returns to stillness.)

END OF PLAY

COSTUMES

The play takes place in the 1990s, and the dress should reflect this. The lawyers of Donne & Russo are a stylish bunch, and dress to look competitive with larger and better known urban law firms — high-end designer wear. The only exception is in Act II, Scene 3, when they are called into the Partner's Lounge from their casual weekend activities. They wear whatever they had on when the emergency meeting was called.

SETTINGS

There are many "locations" in this play. They needn't be rendered in naturalistic detail. In two initial productions, it worked well to have an unmoving backdrop or "environmental presence" (cacti, scrub plants, distant mountains) emblematic of the Southwest, and easily-moved furniture "inside" this picture to define each setting (an office desk/ computer with a chair or two for visitors represents an office, a bed and TV are the Act I, Scene 1 hotel room, a simple table and chair at each end for the Taube's kitchen; simple, elegant, expressive).

The trickiest setting is the final "split" set, comprising "The Wells" and "The Partner's Meeting Hall." I suggest dividing the stage crosswise into two planes, upstage and downstage, using light to emphasize the two areas.

The "rear" set is the Partner's Meeting Hall, with a long table (possibly raised a bit) running left to right and chairs behind for the partners. When they exit the meeting they go offstage left or right, and may then "enter" The Wells from either side downstage.

The "front" setting ("The Wells") has several tables at the side where they won't block the view of the Partner's Meeting Hall behind, but not too far to the side to make the later scenes between Abe, Bennett, Christine and Margot at these table hard to focus. There might be a jukebox somewhere. When action shifts to The Wells, the Partner's Meeting Hall falls dark behind, and partners freeze into shadowy silhouettes. When the action shifts back to the Partrner's Meeting Hall, lights dim in The Wells, which becomes a neutral space between audience and Meeting Hall. Characters in The Wells can drift to the sides of the stage and wait quietly until their set is again the active one.

One moment might break this convention briefly: Bennett's speech. I suggest you might play with the idea that as his speech proceeds, he moves downstage through The Wells (with special lighting) and addresses the audience fully downstage center before moving back into the "real" scene upstage.

Michael Weller
May 14, 2001

Samuel French Theater Bookshops

Specializing in plays and books on theater

45 West 25th Street
Second Floor
New York, NY 10010-2751
212 206 8990/FAX 212 206 1429

7623 Sunset Boulevard
Hollywood, CA 90046-2795
323 876 0570/FAX 323 876 6822

11963 Ventura Boulvard
Studio City, CA 91604-2607
818 762 0535

100 Lombard Street (Lower Level)
Toronto, Ontario M5C 1M3
CANADA
416 363 3536
FAX 416 363 1108

52 Fitzroy Street
London W1T 5JR
ENGLAND
011 44 20 7387 9373
FAX 011 44 20 7387 2161

e-mail: samuelfrench@earthlink.net   website: samuelfrench.com

ISBN 0 573 62817 3   #423